T0194003

GOT MY OWN SONG TO SING

POST-TRAUMATIC SLAVE SYNDROME IN MY FAMILY

JAY THOMAS WILLIS

GOT MY OWN SONG TO SING
POST-TRAUMATIC SLAVE SYNDROME IN MY FAMILY

iUniverse books may be ordered through booksellers or by contacting:

iUniverse
1663 Liberty Drive
Bloomington, IN 47403
www.iuniverse.com
1-800-Authors (1-800-288-4677)

Because of the dynamic nature of the Internet, any web addresses or links contained in this book may have changed since publication and may no longer be valid. The views expressed in this work are solely those of the author and do not necessarily reflect the views of the publisher, and the publisher hereby disclaims any responsibility for them.

Any people depicted in stock imagery provided by Getty Images are models, and such images are being used for illustrative purposes only.
Certain stock imagery © Getty Images.

ISBN: 978-1-5320-9887-1 (sc)
ISBN: 978-1-5320-9888-8 (e)

Library of Congress Control Number: 2020909445

Print information available on the last page.

iUniverse rev. date: 05/27/2020

Contents

Part I
Why My Family Was Dysfunctional

Part II
My Mother Became Paranoid, My Father Punked Out, and My Family Fell Apart

Dedication

To Erma Jean Darden.

"I'm tired of playing music for other folks. I wanna' play a song for me. Got my own song to play."

                     ---- From "Roots," by Alex Haley

"God grant me the serenity to accept the things I cannot change; courage to change the things I can; and the wisdom to know the difference."

                     ---- St. Francis of Asissi

"We see the world not the way it is, but based on how we've been conditioned to see it; it's hard to deliver us from our initial conditioning."

                     ----Jay Thomas Willis

"You must prioritize those things in your life which will aid in your development, and remove those things that are a hindrance to your development."

                     ---- Anonymous

Preface

In this book I tried to point out how the Post-Traumatic Slave Syndrome can be a pathological condition. This condition resulted in some of the negative behavior of African Americans—caused by treatment prior to, during, and after slavery. It consists of both conscious and subconscious behavior, and can range from rather innocuous behavior to serious pathological mental illness.

In this book I refer to the phrase Post-Traumatic Slave Syndrome as being the psychic trauma and conditioning which Blacks were exposed during pre-slavery, slavery, the Middle Passage, post-slavery, and modern times. Though it's called Post-Traumatic Slave Syndrome it refers also to the treatment of Blacks many years before slavery and their continuous treatment and conditioning many years after slavery.

I put forth an example of the Post-Traumatic Slave Syndrome using my family as a case in point. I demonstrate how pre-slavery, Middle Passage, post-slavery, and present-day conditions have contributed to this Post-Traumatic Slave Syndrome being presently manifested and exhibited in my family and other Black families.

I point out pathologies that resulted from these historical conditions as I see them. Blacks were conditioned by chaos, confusion, mistreatment, abuse, and disorganization; and this in some cases likely resulted in psychological problems such as lack of trust, lack of loyalty, lack of love, lack of unity, social and psychological impotence with respect to family, abandonment of family, inability to consolidate resources, excessive drinking, philandering, lack of family values, and a number of other problems in the Black family. These conditions can be traced directly to the Post-Traumatic Slave Syndrome.

I give a detailed explanation of how conditioning during these periods likely contributed to such historical pathologies. It is inconceivable that anything other than the Post-Traumatic Slave Syndrome could have had such a deleterious impact on Black families. Even after all these years this syndrome is still blatantly demonstrating its power in the African American family. This syndrome will likely continue to influence the Black family into the near and distance future.

Acknowledgment

I give thanks to the one and only Almighty God.

ALSO BY JAY THOMAS WILLIS

Nonfiction

A Penny for Your Thoughts: Insights, Perceptions, and Reflections on the African American Condition

Implications for Effective Psychotherapy with African Americans

Freeing the African-American's Mind

God or Barbarian: The Myth of a Messiah Who Will Return to Liberate Us

Finding Your Own African-Centered Rhythm

When the Village Idiot Get Started

Nowhere to Run or Hide

Why Blacks Behave as They Do: The Conditioning Process from Generation to Generation

God, or Balance in the Universe

Over the Celestial Wireless

Paranoid but not Stupid

Nothing but a Man

Prologue

There're reasons why an exceedingly large percentage of the prison population is Black, when Blacks are only approximately 13 percent of the total U.S. population; why a large percentage of Black men abandoned our families; why a great number of Black families are headed by single females; why too many young Black men are involved in homicides and drive-bys; why many young Blacks find escape through drugs and alcohol; why too many Blacks end up in mental institutions; why there is still a high percentage of teenage pregnancies; why Blacks can't seem to achieve a high level of economic development in our communities; and why so many are unemployed and others not looking for a job.

It's felt that the reasons can in part be found in the fact that we were conditioned to negativity during the pre-slavery, Middle Passage, slavery, post-slavery, and present-day periods. We were conditioned during these periods to chaos, confusion, and disorganization; to lack love for ourselves and one another, to lack unity, to lack loyalty, and away from consolidating resources. This has caused us to have self-hate, inferiority feelings, ashamed of our physical characteristics, to lack self-esteem, to lack self-worth, low self-image, lack self-confidence, perform below standards, seek out demeaning relationships, fear disapproval, become alcoholic, sink into depression, have severe emotional problems, lack a sufficient level of motivation, lack of self-identity, and to be destructive toward one another, etc. Our conditioning has caused us to exhibit the negative behavior that can be presently observed in our families.

In the made for television movie "Roots," and in the book by Alex Haley with the same name, when the character Fiddler was getting old, sick, and weak; he and the character Kunta Kinte—the main character, were alone sitting by the rather large roots of an old tree. Fiddler and Kunta both were slaves who had endured many trials and tribulations. Fiddler was used to playing music for others to dance and enjoy. He picked up his fiddle and said, "I'm tired of playing music for other folks. I wanna' play a song for me. Got my own song to play." This book is considered my own song. In this book I tell about my family situation as it relates to the Post-Traumatic Slave Syndrome.

My contention is that pre-slavery, the Middle Passage, slavery, post-slavery, and modern-day conditions all had dysfunctional effects on my family, and so many other families. I will attempt to elaborate in this book how I saw this as taking place in my family. I realize that you can't blame every Black family's problems on these conditions, but I can't help but believe that this situation was contributory to my family's dysfunction. Some individuals choose to blame every problem in the Black family on history.

The first half of the book deals with what happened in the past to lead up to my family's situation and some other Black families' situation. The second half of the book discusses the dysfunction in my family, how it manifested itself, and will continue to manifest itself across the generations. What happened yesterday continues to write on the slate of today (Akbar, 1984, *Chains and Images of Psychological Slavery*).

Some of my sisters and brothers were raised during the Depression and World War II. Things were scarce during this time. My parents came from the old school, and continued to raise the children in the old tradition. Though, my parents' approach to raising the children were dysfunctional, my family was so isolated that the same old tradition was continued. In addition, there were alcohol, mental illness, philandering, and other problems. Out of this situation ten children were born and raised, and most but not all turned out to be dysfunctional. It is felt that at least part of this dysfunction came out of my family's history.

Even some erudite scholars have a hard time understanding how historical conditioning has affected the Black family. Some scholars say the Black family was doing better many years ago when discrimination, bigotry, and prejudice were fully operational. There are those who will say that such dysfunction could not have persisted throughout the years without some inherent-internal factors that are genetic to the Black family, and besides Black families were doing better many years ago when there was more discrimination. Why is the Black family now suddenly in a more difficult situation? Thomas Sowell in *Wealth, Poverty, and Politics* (2015); and, Reginald G. Damerell in *Education's Smoking Gun* (1985), posed the idea that if the problems in the Black family are a legacy of slavery, why then in the early 1900s was the Black illegitimacy rate a tiny fraction of today's rate? Roughly 75%, and in New York City 85% of Black children lived in two parent households. It is suggested that crime rates and rates of poverty have increased from an earlier period. There are many variables these factors could be based on. If this is true, families are in more distress at a time when we are subjected to less discrimination, something must be wrong with this picture. This doesn't necessarily suggest that today's rate of illegitimacy and weak family structure has nothing to do with discrimination or slavery. Maybe the moral climate of the country has changed. It could also be that if left to fester like a sore the situation will likely get worse exponentially over a period of time. Problems would seem to get better over time, but if nothing is done to improve them, the problems will increase. Also, if the conditions are reinforced on a daily basis, the conditions will likely get worse. The situation is like burning embers hidden under ashes; the embers will burn underneath the ashes, and erupt at a later point if tampered with, always burning just beneath the surface.

The ideas in this book come not from what my parents had to say but from my parents' behavior. The Black family structure being dysfunctional is by design. Its history and present conditions have made it dysfunctional. This dysfunction has been perpetuated upon Blacks in order to accomplish a long-range plan of genocide. There has been a long-term conspiracy to remove Black people from the face of the Earth. Other groups took us from Africa many years ago against our will. Then these groups wanted to return them to Africa after slavery (Bennett, 1999, *Forced into Glory: Abraham Lincoln's White Dream*). Now that we have further outlived what others see as our useful purpose, other groups want to get rid of us again (Wilhelm, 1970, *Who needs the Negro?*), like an orange once you have squeezed out all the juice. In the meantime, other groups have inflicted every manner of deprivation, genocide, discrimination, racism, prejudice, and bigotry that could be perpetuated upon a people. The only way to stop a conspiracy is to expose it.

It has been noted all over the world that the family is the basic unit in any society. This being the case, it stands to reason that in order for either the individual or the community to be strong, the family must be strong. If the family as a unit is dealt a severe blow, then the individual and the community will feel the effects. Since the African American family was not a functional entity during slavery, in spite of what Gutman (1976) says in *The Black Family in Slavery and Freedom 1750-1925*, as well as what some others had to say about the functioning of the family during slavery; it is felt that there is very little evidence to say that the family was strong during this period (less one gets into semantics about the definition of strong), by standard definitions of what constitutes a strong family, the African American family certainly wasn't strong during this period. In most cases the African American community defers to standard definitions and concepts unless it is convenient to do otherwise. It can be said that every effort was made to destroy the African American family. It can be witnessed that in spite of this effort, perpetrators were not completely successful. Since there is little evidence to say that the African American family has ever been a strong entity in this country, one may understand why there has been little effort to act collectively on the part of African Americans. After all, if one's family does not perform as a collective unit, why should there be motivation to perform as a collective with others. If one does not have a strong family, then there is no spirit to work toward anything collectively that might improve the situation of African Americans as a whole, even if this means achieving some fundamental freedoms. From the basic family unit which works to protect and nourish the individual comes the collective spirit, without this one does not have the basis for any cohesive effort, all that one can know is ingratiation through self-interest (Kardiner and Ovesey, 1962, in *The Mark of Oppression*).

Trauma is usually a violent injury caused by an external physical, psychological or spiritual assault, force, event, or experience. This trauma can upset one's balance and sense of stability. A severe trauma can distort one's perspectives. This often results in dysfunctional attitudes, behaviors, and beliefs, which can in-turn produce adjustment issues. One severe trauma can produce such results, if this pattern is multiplied, devastation of the individual can result. These traumas are much worse when caused by human beings (Degruy, 2005, *Post Traumatic Slave Syndrome: America's Legacy of Enduring Injury and Healing*). The effects of this trauma and dehumanization are still prevalent in the behavior of Blacks today, and can be explained by the idea of a Post-Traumatic Slave Syndrome.

Post-Traumatic Slave Syndrome is a condition that developed in a population that has experienced multi-generational trauma. It results from centuries of slavery and continuous exposure to oppression and institutional racism today. In addition, this condition is a real or imagined beliefs that the benefits of the society in which a people live are not accessible (Degruy, 2005, *Post Traumatic Slave Syndrome: America's Legacy of Enduring Injury and Healing*).

Slavery initiated stressors that were devastating, creating a sore on the Black American's psyche that continues to raise its ugly head. Human beings react and experience trauma differently. Some people are not traumatized by traumatic events. But it's definite that Black Americans in general suffer from Post-Traumatic Slave Syndrome. Black Americans have experienced a legacy of slavery. This legacy of trauma is reflected in many of their behaviors and beliefs; behaviors and beliefs that at one time were necessary to adopt in order to survive, yet today serve to undermine their ability to be successful. The Post-Traumatic Slave Syndrome has impacted the lives of untold Black Americans. Being told you are inhuman for many years and treated like an animal can have a definite psychic impact on one's behavior, impacts that are passed on from one generation to another. Most Blacks bear the burden of our ancestors to some degree. Some of us bear it more than others; most of us have been impacted in some way. Many years of slavery and oppression certainly has affected many Black Americans.

The purpose of this book is to gain a greater understanding of the impact many years of slavery and oppression had on my family and other Black families. In too many cases today's Black mothers, fathers, and children don't understand the historical forces that helped to shape our behavior. This book sheds light on that subject.

PART I

Why My Family Was Dysfunctional

"How you see things is how you have been taught to see them."
----Jay Thomas Willis

"We are at the bottom of society because we have become disconnected from our spirituality."
----Anonymous

"A man can be conditioned to accomplish almost any objective, if the conditioning is severe enough."
----Jay Thomas Willis

"It is difficult to be productive when you live in filth, disease, and desperation."
----Jay Thomas Willis

"If you have no resources you have no options."
----Jay Thomas Willis

1

―――――――――― ⋆ ――――――――――

Pre-Slavery's Contribution to My Family's Dysfunction

It is felt that most of the well-known present and past problems of the Black family originate from its having been assaulted—physically and mentally—for many years (Du Bois, 1990, *The world and Africa*; Clarke, 1991, *Notes for an African World Revolution: Africans at the Crossroads*; Williams, 1987, *The Destruction of Black Civilization*; Grier & Cobbs, 1980, *Black Rage*; Diop, 1991, *Civilization or Barbarism*; Jackson, 1970, *Introduction to African Civilization*; Franklin, 1988, *From Slavery to Freedom: A History of Negro Americans* 6th ed.; Windsor, 1988, *From Babylon to Timbuktu*; deGraft-Johnson, 1986, *African Glory*). This war upon Blacks and our culture have brought about the Post-Traumatic Slave Syndrome. This syndrome is manifested by the fact that no matter what individuals may achieve educationally, economically, socially, or politically; these individuals are predisposed to act at some point, sooner or later, in a manner that is destructive to themselves or others. Few escape this detrimental process and only to a variable extent.

Blacks were unconsciously programmed from our first contact with other groups to become vulnerable to the Post-Traumatic Slave Syndrome. We have continued to be programmed on a daily basis to manifest this Post-Traumatic Slave Syndrome. After having been programmed for this Syndrome, many Blacks will either become negative in our behavior in some way: seek out a relationship with someone who is likely to extirpate us, or find a specific vice that will ultimately prove deleterious. In many cases, these behaviors can occur separately or simultaneously for any one individual. We also must realize that this Post-Traumatic Slave Syndrome can be manifested in many different ways. For example, suicide, drug abuse, homicide, destructive relationships, ethical-professional problems, gambling, perverse-sexual behavior, and a variety of other negative behaviors, are just a few of the many ways in which this behavior can be displayed.

The Black story represents one of the greatest survival stories of Earth's history. For us to experience the cruelty, brutality, and wickedness we encountered, and survive the experience with any amount of collective or individual sanity is a near-miracle. However, that survival experience did not occur without its consequences. In fact, there were many long-lasting consequences which continue to effect Blacks today (Williams, 1991, *They Stole it but You Must Return it*).

This Post-Traumatic Slave Syndrome began to manifest itself many years before the slave trade and continues to the present-day. When other groups invaded Africa, they took control of the various institutions and began to dismantle them. African social organizations were restructured by other groups. Other groups were successful at instigating infighting among the various tribes. "Other groups' conquest changed power relations within African society. Commodity exchange and materialism now became attractive incentives for Africans to kill and help capture other Africans" (Hutchinson, 1990, p. 3, *The mugging of Black America*). While the various African groups were fighting each other, other foreign groups took total control of our people and resources. "Most of the visitors to Africa and the invaders were first accepted as friends because, in most cases, the Africans thought their intentions were good. The invaders stayed on in Africa as conquerors and enslavers, and most of the visitors stayed on as their collaborators" (Clarke, 1991, p. 135, *Notes for an African World Revolution: Africans at the Crossroads*). Africans trusted other groups to make decisions, and to select those who would make decisions. This process was continued throughout Africa by other groups. African values were seen as inferior, and an attempt was made to replace them with the values of other groups. A new standard was set for the Africans by other groups. Other groups were ardent explorers, and generally left their women behind. They had a habit of taking women as concubines wherever they went. They therefore took African women as concubines and sometimes married them. When offspring came from the marriage, the offspring generally took the side of their fathers, which gave the fathers leverage, but was not always in the best interest of African culture. This further contributed to the breakdown of African culture and society. This gave other groups more influence in the tribe and the structure of the family. The African women were only used to gain the necessary control. Consequently, much of the history and culture of the Africans were destroyed.

Africans were invaded many times. Each time the invaders left the society worse off than it was previously. Other groups came to pilfer and destroy, having no respect for African culture. This was the genesis of the Post-Traumatic Slave Syndrome. Once family and tribal structures became weakened, and after long periods of physical and mental abuse, Africans were automatically programmed for this negativity. The psyche of individuals was affected by the widespread dismantling of African culture and institutions. After confiscating the natural resources, manipulating the men and women, replacing the African's god, and inflicting a severe blow to the language and culture, Africans were left with nothing to sustain ourselves and our culture. This left Africans totally confused, made it possible for other groups to initiate the slave trade, and for it to meet with little resistance (Clarke, 1991, *Notes for an African World Revolution: Africans at the Crossroads*). Once the Africans' basic institutions were tampered with, we had no strong foundation on which to base our behavior: at that point, our behavior became purposeless, aimless, and chaotic. Africans soon forgot our own history, culture, and roots. After many such invasions, we began to manifest this negative syndrome.

Before other groups invaded Africa, in some places we enjoyed harmonious families, advanced education, well-organized governments, productive economics, and a strong base, which led to high moral values. Africa was a beautiful green landscape with plush forest and many animals. It had surpassed the world in scholarship and learning. Suggest Latif and Latif (1994) in *Slavery: the African American Psychic Trauma*.

Other groups began to explore other parts of the world many years ago. It was then that other groups set foot on the African continent, according to Clarke (1991), in *Notes for an African World Revolution: Africans at the Crossroads*. This is where our problems seemingly began. Everybody should know that Africans have been distraught since the first outsider set foot on the continent. We know that various groups have since that time exploited African institutions and resources. The Europeans weren't the first foreigners to appear on the continent. The first Europeans appeared when Alexander invaded the continent about 332 B.C.

My thesis is that what happened to the African family many years ago has partially caused the Black family of today to be conditioned to dysfunction. Africans were first invaded by a number of other groups, who did so successively (Williams, 1987, *The Destruction of Black Civilization*). Other groups had existed on the African continent prior to their separation many years before. It has been suggested that all intelligent life, as we know it began on the African continent. Other groups left and populated other parts of the world. How they left and came by populating other parts of the world is difficult to say. It was many years ago when other groups began to explore that they rediscovered the African continent. African's were subsequently under constant siege. The Africans were invaded by the Hebrews, the Greeks, the Arabians, the Persians, the Assyrians, the Portuguese, the Romans, and others; as suggested by Williams (1987), in *The Destruction of Black Civilization*. Clarke also noted this fact in many of his numerous lectures and books. Yosef ben-Johannan (1971) came to a similar conclusion in his book, *Africa: Mother of Western Civilization*. Some invasions lasted for a long period and others for short periods. Africans were friendly toward these groups and invited them into their homes, families, and societies. We also allowed them to become part of our family structure. As John Henrik Clarke once said in one of his many lectures, "We are always inviting people to lunch, and end up becoming the lunch." We invited other groups to lunch in Africa many years ago when they first arrived on the continent, and we've become the proverbial entrée—there and everywhere else in the world since that time. We invited other groups into our society and gave them every amenity that we enjoyed. Subsequently, they infiltrated the African society and it has been on the decline ever since. Because of our gentle and trusting nature, other groups took control of the resources they could use and began a process of destruction of what was not useful to them. Blacks have become the symbolic lunch of the world. This is because we now produce for everybody but ourselves and take care of everybody but our own. We're the only people who help build nations yet have no ownership or interest in what was built.

Each invasion deteriorated the Africans' institutions, culture, and left us worse off than we were before. Once inside our society other groups proceeded to systematically dismantle the structure of the Africans' institutions, after they convinced the Africans that other groups' values and culture were superior and Africans' culture inferior (Williams, 1987, *The Destruction of Black Civilization*). Africans assumed these individuals had good intentions. In many cases other groups were put in control or had direct access to someone in control. Once this occurred the individuals in power began to change the makeup of the various institutions. By the time the other groups had finished they had dismantled the social, political, economic, educational and familial institutions of Africans. Years of interference from outside cultures destroyed the very basis for African society, and we tried to replace it with other groups' institutions and values. Neither the Black family nor African society has been the same since. Africans were subsequently conditioned to self-hate, feeling our culture and characteristics were indeed inferior. These changes created havoc, chaos, and confusion that have been internalized and passed on from generation to generation. Since that time other groups have maintained powerful influences which keep Blacks divided and in turmoil. The African society had been all but destroyed to the extent that we were vulnerable to the slave trade. Africans misunderstood other cultures, and other cultures misunderstood Africans. Once societal structures were changed there was a loss of traditional norms and values with no sense of clear directions for the future. This resulted in confusion over what was acceptable, moral, and reasonable. Such situations are natural for breeding normlessness and conflict. When Africans became confused, chaotic, and disgruntled; we turned on each other, because our fellow tribesman made a readily available target. The ones directly responsible for the conflict weren't always available targets. We took everything thrown at us and turned the hostility, anger, and frustration right back at one another (Wilson, video, "Blue Print for Black Power.").

Alexander the Great contributed to breakdown of the African culture. Alexander was noted to have looted and burned a number of libraries in Egypt that were important sources of knowledge for the world.

He gave books to his Greek friends that they then used for their own purposes, suggested James (1988), in *Stolen Legacy*. Napoleon also looted museums, temples and other places, distributing artifacts to European museums. Note that temples were often used as libraries as well as spiritual places in those days. Other groups then said Africa had no written tradition. Also, others helped to destroy Black culture and history, and told Blacks we had no history that was noteworthy. Blacks were also told we hadn't contributed anything noteworthy to world civilization and culture (Williams, 1987, *The Destruction of Black Civilization*). These books contained the highest development of knowledge in the world at that time. In actuality Africans contributed the basis for what would become modern science, technology, medicine, architecture, agriculture, astronomy, and mathematics. For example, Socrates was given credit for the maxim *Know Thyself*, when it had obviously been inscribed over an Egyptian temple long before Alexander invaded Egypt. James also noted that Socrates was given credit for having instructed Plato in some areas in which he had no personal knowledge. Plato had to get his information from some other source, such as the books written by Egyptians scholars. Again, James suggests that there is no way Plato and other Greek scholars could have written the books they were given credit. These books were written by Egyptian scholars and given to Greek scholars by Alexander the Great. The Greek scholars were seemingly guilty of plagiarism.

Before Alexander the Great, great Black empires had ruled Africa. Long before other groups came to Africa, there were the great empires of Benin, Songhai, Gao, Mali, Timbuktu, and Ghana, etc. Timbuktu was the major center of learning for all Africa. It was populated with thousands of scholars and wise men seeking to increase their knowledge. These cities had farmers, artisans, blacksmiths, tanners, dyers, and weavers. In addition, there were much trading and commerce. Tradesman gathered to buy goods with gold. Some of the biggest merchants sold nothing but parchments and books. Most of the knowledge came from Timbuktu. Many see

Africa as too primitive for such activities at that time. The coming of other groups signaled the decline of African civilization rather than its advance (Williams, 1987, *The Destruction of Black Civilization*). When other groups came to Africa they were seen as superior. Africans were conditioned to feel inferior by their treatment since others arrived in Africa. Today Africans are still plagued by feelings of inferiority. Invading countries only had their own interest in mind. It is believed that there was something in the African folklore that indicated a bearded god would return from across the seas to become our leader and save us from our decadent plight. When other groups came the Africans were chickens ready to be plucked. A similar notion existed in the culture of the North and South American Indians, as well as some other cultures. How this notion became a part of these groups' folklore is anybody's guess. But other groups have a similar notion in their perspective of a "Second Coming" that we are all familiar with. Some believe a blue-eyed, blonde, bearded god will come back to save them from themselves. So, this idea is not so farfetched.

We know that many years later after being successively invaded by a number of different cultures the African culture had been dealt a severe blow. After other group's influence broke down the African culture for many years, our culture was so denigrated, confused, and disorganized that it was ripe for the slave trade. As Walter Rodney (1972) indicates in How *Europe Underdeveloped Africa*, Europe had begun the process of under developing Africa. When the slave trade came along Africans were highly vulnerable, simply too disorganized, and didn't have the wherewithal to defend themselves. In addition, our technology was underdeveloped. Other groups were better organized and had superior weapons. The Africans could not match the superior firepower of these other groups. Others could kill hundreds of natives before the Africans could kill a few of them. These groups had weapons made of forged steel. The Africans had weapons, but were crude sticks sharpened to a point at the end, crude bow and arrows, and shields made of straws and strings. The Africans fought very gallant battles, but in the end could no longer stand the superior firepower, and took up residence in the hills and jungles. After many successive invasions, African societies had been weakened over many years.

When the slave trade came along our institutions and culture had been too severely dismantled to fight against it. Our social, economic, political, religious, and familial institutions had all been broken down. The Africans had been reduced to a bunch of separate tribes and clans—with no unity. It was easy for other groups to enslave the Africans, or do whatever they wanted with us, because we had lost the basis for our existence—our sense of culture and values. For a drink of whiskey, a piece of red cloth, or a trinket of some kind, we sold each other out. And we were sitting on gold, diamonds, and many other minerals and resources that we didn't know what to do with. Before we knew what was happening, we found ourselves in chains and on our way to the ships waiting on the shore.

Africans were mostly a bunch of disorganized tribes and clans scattered throughout the hills and jungles. There was little unity or loyalty among any of the Africans. Any other tribe or clan was seen as an enemy rather than an ally. If one clan or tribe was attacked, most often another clan felt no necessity to fight with or for it. It's kind of like Africa has been recently: we have been too busy fighting one another. Each country has no alliances with other countries. In fact, other countries are often seen as an enemy. Too often there are tribes and clans within each country who are fighting each other, not to mention fighting with other countries within Africa. Other groups were frequently able to manipulate tribes and clans into even more warfare than was ordinary.

Before the slave trade, Africans had always been vulnerable to outside forces, because we lacked a sufficient standing army with the necessary technology and sufficient unity. There are approximately 58 countries in Africa, from 700 to 3,000 languages, and many more dialects and cultures. These things along with vast territory, and many natural barriers, made it difficult for Africans to unite. Many of the cultures clashed in terms of ideology and were even further divided. We ended up fighting each other rather than uniting against outside forces that threatened us. That is another reason it was so easy to manage the slave trade; and for other countries to take control of land, minerals and other resources. After the slave trade, major countries divided Africa's resources. Once Africa had been invaded and conquered many times, forced to accept many different cultural values; and having our best and brightest stolen from us, we didn't know if we were literally coming or going.

It is difficult to say when my family's problems began. Our problems probably began when the first group of foreigners set foot on the shore of Africa over many years ago. The problems continued with slavery. In slavery and after slavery my ancestors were some of those who weren't able to develop economic, social, political, psychological, and educational situations. My subsequent ancestors had problems because of this history, as did many other families. Such conditions were passed on to my great-great-great-grandparents, then to my grandparents, and then on to my parents, and my parents simply passed it along to the children. My parents had this syndrome because of family's history. I am the way I am because of my parent's history.

Our disunity, disloyalty, self-hate, lack of group consciousness, and other dysfunctions, didn't just begin in slavery. I debated with a fellow colleague once while teaching at a Southern university that Black problems began in slavery, this was before I expanded my reading habits. I hadn't thought to look for causes prior to slavery. Even though I had attended many lectures and received several degrees, I still didn't realize this fact. My colleague was right, because our problems began when other groups first set foot on the African continent. They say if all you know about African history is what happened in slavery, you know nothing about Black history. My orientation was limited at the time to what happened in slavery.

Blacks were conditioned by this time to a lack of unity, a sense of impotence, lack of group consciousness, and disorganization. This situation also disorganized the family structure and conditioned Blacks to self-hate.

2

ርፄ✦ፄጋ

How the Middle Passage Contributed to My Family's Dysfunction

A harmonious community was shattered by foreign invaders who kidnapped many of its citizens. We were suddenly attacked, handcuffed, and dragged away in the night. We were filled with fear, abatement, confusion, hopelessness, and despair. Supremacist would later call this a blessing in disguise, for the Africans were being saved from the savagery of Africa. We were later told we were rescued from this savage land for our own good, and that other groups brought civilization to this uncivilized land. Latif and Latif (1994) refers to this situation as a crisis of identity, in *Slavery: The African American Psychic Trauma*.

The Middle Passage describes the journey that brought slaves from West Africa to the New World. The Middle Passage describes one leg of the triangular route of trade that brought captured Africans to the Americas and enslaved us. Africans were marched in chains across miles of difficult terrain after being apprehended somewhere in West Africa. Men, women and children were placed in chains and delivered at gunpoint to waiting slave ships where we were marched to the Western seaboard. Millions were forced onto cargo ships bound for unknown lands that included Brazil, the West Indies, Europe, the United States, and some other countries. Many of us died en route to the coast while trying to resist our enslavers, some died during the initial stage of the voyage, and others died after reaching the Americas. Our deaths and suffering are relevant because of the impression left on the Africans who were able to observe the process.

Africans were snatched from our homeland, without a clue as to where we were being taken. After being captured by one means or another, sometimes sold out by members of one's own tribe, at other times captured in hard-fought battles; we became too weak to defend ourselves. Too often we were captured because we were too trustworthy. In any regard, it was a long, barefoot-thorny trek across miles of rough terrain to get to the ships that awaited us. We were driven in chains like cattle across this terrain to get to the ships. We suffered much abuse from our captors, and were forced to move on no matter the conditions or how we felt (Ransford, 1971, *The Slave Trade*). During this trek, many Africans died in going from their homes to ships on the coast. Some were killed, some died of starvation, many died because the trip was too brutal, while others simply gave up and refused to move. Many died on this trek across the landscape: because of harsh treatment and outright murder. We were separated and chained from the beginning to the end of the trip, and could do little about our condition, since we were overpowered. In most cases there were few means of escape. We were beaten and abused every step of this journey.

It was easy to capture the Africans for the slave trade. All others had to do was demonstrate their superior firepower by killing a few, and the rest would disband and give up. Not to mention these groups frequently had help from other Africans. Without adequate technology it's difficult for a group to defend itself. If a group can't adequately engage in self-defense, it's left open to be taken advantage of. This transatlantic slave voyage between Africa and the Americas claimed the lives of approximately 1.8 million slaves over a period of about 250 years. Some say that more died than were killed in the Jewish holocaust. The number transported has been estimated differently by different sources, from a few million by some to as high as 100 million by others. Many died as reached the end of the voyage. Many died fighting on the way to the slave ships. The actual number who died in the voyages will likely remain untold. This was a 1,500 miles ocean voyage across turbulent seas. The Middle Passage was a physical and psychological nightmare for an estimated 12 million slaves, who were packed like animals, aboard slave vessels. It was a terrifying experience. The conditions were deplorable and miserable (Robison, 1999, *Africana: The Encyclopedia of the African American Experience*, p. 1302).

Slaves were usually shackled in pairs, the right arm and leg of one was chained to the left leg and arm of the other. We were separated according to language, culture, and tribe. We were confined below deck and packed into "slave quarters" throughout the ship's belly. We were stuffed in the holds of ships in quarters that were no more than six-feet long and not high enough to allow an individual to sit upright; much as sardines are packed in a can, in a way to fit as many as possible, and treated like animals—for many months of voyage. Slaves were forced to lie naked on wooden planks, and many developed bruises and open sores. The unbearable heat below deck, mixed with the human waste and vomit, produced an overpowering stench. Many of us died lying in our own excrement or the excrement of others. We sometimes slept next to others who had died because we could not stand the filth. The unsanitary conditions were breeding grounds for diseases like dysentery, smallpox, flux, and measles; and there was all manner of other diseases. Close to 5 percent of the slaves died from diseases, and many more from malnutrition. Many were murdered for failure to comply with orders (Robinson, 1999, Africana: *The Encyclopedia of the African American Experience*, p. 1302).

We were packed in the holds of ships like animals going to the market, chained and stacked three and four abreast on iron cots with little air, water, food or appropriate clothing. Africans were loaded onto ships and crammed together with sometimes less than 18 inches between them. If the Africans protested, we were beaten, flogged, hung, or tossed overboard as examples to the others (Hutchinson, 1990, *The Mugging of Black America*). The heat was overwhelming, and some slaves died of suffocation while remaining chained to those yet living. Diseases, which were often fatal (smallpox, dysentery, and other viral diseases), were prevalent among the slaves. Many died of melancholia or suicide. The slave was simply thrown overboard if he or she became deathly ill. Also, in some cases when there was an acute outbreak of a disease, ships were sometimes abandoned with their human cargo chained helpless in the holds, destined to suffer a slow merciless death. The physical environment of men and women on the ships were similar (Goode, 1969, *From Africa to the United States and then….*; Ransford, 1971, *The Slave Trade*; Howard, 1971, *Black Voyage*; Franklin, 1988, *From Slavery to Freedom: A History of Negro Americans*). We existed this way for many weeks to several months in the holds of the ship. We were without human contact but shared in each other's collective misery. We slept, wept, ate, defecated, urinated, menstruated, vomited, gave birth, and died in the same area (Degruy, 2005, *Post Traumatic Slave Syndrome: America's Legacy of Enduring Injury and Healing).* Those who lived through these experiences had profound memories, which were passed on to future generations. This treatment served to add to the Post-Traumatic Slave Syndrome that we are witnessing today.

We existed in these conditions for many months at a time. If a ship feared capture by the authorities the whole cargo would sometimes be thrown overboard. We were fed twice a day rations of fish, beans, mush, or yams. Those who refuse to eat, hoping to starve to death, were force-fed. Slaves were periodically allowed to come on deck for exercises in small groups and to get fresh air. Women and children were frequently permitted to roam freely and were often raped or abused by the ship's crew. There were occasional mutinies. Some slaves either starved or hanged themselves; some jumped overboard. Slaves who resisted their captors were killed; others took their own lives rather than be resigned to a life of cruelty and torture (Robinson, 1999, *Africana: The Encyclopedia of the African American Experience*, p. 1302).

Many never saw any of their family members again. Those who lived passed on our experiences, and carried our psychological scars to our graves. Again, we were mistreated, abused, and misused every step of the journey.

The first African captives were brought to Portugal in 1644. The first slaves brought to North America were in 1619, almost 400 years ago. Slavery has existed in human history for a long time, but America's particular brand of chattel slavery represents a case of human trauma incomparable in scope, duration, and consequences to any other incidence of human bondage (Degruy, 2005, *Post Traumatic Slave Syndrome: America's Legacy of Enduring Injury and Healing*).

Latif and Latif (1994*) in Slavery: The African American Psychic Trauma* further states, captives were smuggled away, locked in chains, and shipped off to a foreign land, where we were murdered, tortured, raped, beaten, and forced to labor in the fields under the lash of a whip, and the constant threat of death.

We were conditioned to a sense of self-hate and feelings of inferiority through degradation and dehumanization. Also, we were conditioned to impotence and lack of unity, because of our inability to mount a successful collective response. In this experience we were also conditioned to self-hate, lack of unity, and impotence.

3

CUSO

Slavery's Contribution to My Family's Dysfunction

The slave experience was one of unrelenting attacks on the captives' body, mind, and spirit. The captives were traumatized throughout our lives and the attacks persisted long after emancipation. We had to adapt our attitudes and behavior in order to survive, and these adaptations continue to be prevalent in the behavior of Blacks today. Even more impactful than the physical assaults on our bodies was the daily insults to our psyche (Degruy, 2005, in *Post Traumatic Slave syndrome: America's Legacy of Enduring Injury and Healing*).

"Since the capture and transport of the first African slaves, those brought to these shores had to deal with systematic efforts to destroy the bonds of relationships that held us together, as well as continuing efforts to have us believe ourselves to be less than human" (Degruy, 2005, p. 115, *Post Traumatic Slave Syndrome: America's Legacy of Enduring Injury and Healing*).

Any form of bondage is abusive. Slavery could be nothing but abusive and cruel to a human being. Slaves had no rights that the slave owner was bound to respect. The slave master could beat, maim, kill, dismember, work to death, deprive of food and water, whip, rape repeatedly, or any other way of achieving our humiliation; the slave master could do with us whatever they wanted. We were considered less than an animal in the barn and treated worse. Every day of our life was an insult to our dignity, our humanity, and our soul. It was legal to beat, torture, sell, or kill slaves (Degruy, 2005, *Post Traumatic Slave Syndrome: America's Legacy of Enduring Injury and Healing*).

Slavery was a cruel, harsh, and devastating process. The experience of pain, cruelty, and deprivation was rampant. There was oppression of the spirit, loss of hope, loss of self-respect, and loss of dignity experienced by the slaves. Personal choice was nonexistent; there was no protection under the law. All of this was sanctioned by religious, judicial, and military powers (Berry & Blassingame, 1982, *Long Memory*). "Once instituted, the system became self-perpetuating, gathering momentum as it went, and leaving in its wake human beings living a nonhuman existence" (Feldstein, 1971, p. 28, *Once a Slave*). In order to develop an effective slave system, the self-image, self-concept, as well as the family structure had to be destroyed. "The ideal slave had to be absolutely dependent and have a deep consciousness of personal inferiority. Color was made the badge of that degradation" (Grier & Cobbs, 1980, p. 26, *Black Rage*).

There was for many a break-in period in the islands of the Americas. This treatment was even more brutal; slaves were conditioned to be slaves. It was noted that some women had their fetuses cut from their abdomen as a part of this conditioning and dehumanization process. In other cases, slaves were whipped and beaten to condition to servitude in America, and other parts of the world. In slavery, Blacks couldn't vote, were only considered three-fifths a person, and didn't have equal rights as individuals. At the risk of being called a "slavery pimp," I'll say that at least some of our problems did begin in slavery.

In America we were placed on the auction block and sold to the highest bidder. Many slaves were killed, and the slave master didn't have to account for us. They would simply bury the slave in an unmarked grave somewhere in the woods; no one in authority had to be notified. The life of slaves wasn't worth much, because we could be killed at any time—for any reason.

The powers that be never intended for these Africans in America, that other groups stole from Africa, to develop advanced societies and communities. Other groups sought to create a permanent slave class. Those in power united in order to prevent Africans from ever becoming a powerful force in this country. These groups feared retributions from the Africans if we should ever get our act together. The slave master knew that in certain parts of the South slaves outnumbered the slave masters. The slave master also felt if the slave should rebel en masse against the system they would have problems.

The slave master had to condition the slave, so he'd never have the collective resources to rise up against the system. To do that, the slave master had to institute some rigorous conscious and unconscious conditioning.

The first step the slave master used to condition the slave was to dehumanize, humiliate, and to take away all signs of personal identification. The slave was stripped of all clothing and head was shaved. All affiliation, individual status, and personal style were removed. The slave master wanted the slave to be seen as just a "jungle savage" by all who viewed him. It was easier that way. To successfully condition the slave, all resistance to the system had to be crushed. The slave master didn't want anything but a non-person, a body without a brain, a basic slave. He didn't want an office manager, or an administrator. He just wanted a broken African. Those who captured and sold Africans had their agenda well planned. Blacks were forcibly captured, stolen, regularly abused, and beaten into submission over many years.

The second step to successful slave conditioning was to separate the slaves who spoke the same language, had the same culture, or came from the same locality. This was to prevent rebellion, plotting, insurrection, or uprising. The slave usually found another language being spoken by other slaves. African languages, and in many cases, African drums which carried messages were banned. Any writing, of course, was out of the question. Africans were forced to learn another language without benefit of formal schooling in that country. The slave was simply looked upon as being "dumb." This situation has led to their always being communication difficulties between slaves. Even now, when Africans speak the same language, we have difficulty understanding one another—in many cases, from my experiences. The slave usually had to learn another language in a hurry in order to establish communication in a heterogeneous group into which we were thrown. By outlawing teaching a slave to read and write slaveholders were able to convince many slaves that Africans really were less intelligent.

The third step for the successful conditioning of the slave was to instill an overwhelming fear of other groups that the slaves dare not rebel. This was done by the most extreme violence. Constant beatings helped to reinforce the power of the master over the slave. Angry masters frequently kicked, slapped, cuffed, or boxed the ears of the slave. Sometimes the master would flog pregnant women, and often punish slaves so severely that it took us weeks to recover. The slave master would occasionally put iron weights with bells on them placed on our necks. The more the slave rebelled the crueler the punishment. One incorrigible slave received 100 to 200 lashes from his owner; once the owner poured tar on his head and set it on fire; once the master had the nails on his fingers and toes beaten off. Fear of the master was deeply impressed in the minds of slaves. Disobedience might mean torture or death. It was the duty of the slaves to protect the children by instilling fear and obedience to the slave master. Unknowingly, to this day some African American parents teach the children fear of other groups. Other groups in a position of authority had the power to destroy a slave's life if he was displeasured by his show of "impudence." This fear has been passed down too many Blacks from generation to generation. Many common disciplinary practices of African American parents can be traced to the slavery-time philosophy of instilling fear into the child. The child's spirit was broken early as a means of protecting against later possibly fatal punishment from the master.

The fourth step toward successful conditioning of a slave was to breakup the family. Being sold away, or watching family members get sold away, was an indescribably devastating experience. Many slaves became so overwhelmed with grief we went insane. Separating children from parents was perhaps the greatest factor in the loss of African culture and language. Once children were taken away, upbringing was no longer supervised by parents who could pass down knowledge and traditions. Without passing on knowledge and traditions by parents, there's no connection with the past. This leaves only the repulsive image of Africa created by the slave master as a place inhabited by wild men and savages.

The maintenance of healthy and secure relationships are among the most important values within the African culture. If you destroy this ability in an individual you almost destroy the individual. American chattel slavery destroyed existing relationships and undermined the Black American's ability to form healthy new ones.

The fifth step toward successfully conditioning the slave was to not hold marriages sacred. One could be sold away at any time, or the master could take a liking to one's wife. Some masters would breed their slaves for the purpose of getting a desired result. A monogamous family life among the slaves would interfere with such a system. Promiscuity was encouraged among the slaves. The slave master also took liberty with the slave women. In some cases, every man in sight was encouraged to mate with the slaves. All for the purpose of producing more slaves. Some were even paid to mate with the slaves. Slave women were punished if there was any resistance. Black men were powerless to do anything about the situation. Other groups could sexually abuse any slave woman they so desired. This has caused a lack of respect between Black men and women that can be seen even today. It was the woman's sense of dignity and sexual integrity which had to be crushed in order for slavery to be successful. The rape of African women served as an important means of mind control. Forced sexual relations with the slave master had the effect of destroying the slave woman's self-esteem and feelings of personal worth. This created lack of trust among Black men and women. This causes a lack of dependence on one another. The male slave saw himself as being weak an inferior. This caused Black males to compensate by becoming super masculine individuals, who today go from woman to woman, much as occurred on the plantation. Sometimes Black male slaves were hired out to other plantations to impregnate other female slaves. Having little else to be proud of besides his state of powerlessness, sexual prowess became a means whereby a Black male slave could gain status. It is still status today for some Black men to father children by many women. The slave master created distrust among the slaves that is still a factor in the lives of many Blacks.

The sixth step toward successfully conditioning of Blacks was to give them a Christian name and convert them to Christianity. The vast majority of slaves brought to this country were Islamic. Africans were forced to change our original names to Christian names. This helped to destroy cultural, economic, and religious affiliations with specific nations in Africa. The need to convert "heathen" Africans to Christianity was cited as a major justification for the slave trade. Other groups said that once Africans were converted to their version of Christianity, we became more manageable. Religion became a political tool to control the slaves and protect the business interest of those involved in the slave trade. Christianity took Blacks away from our African spirituality and gave us a blonde-headed, blue-eyed savior.

The last step in creating a successful slave trading industry was to convince the next generation of Africans, those born as slaves in America, that it was better to forget a shameful past in Africa. The slave master wanted to maintain or create an image of a "naked jungle savage." Part of the reason for stripping the new arrivals of their clothing was to promote this image. Other groups painted Africa in such graphically grotesque pictures: a place where Blacks cannibals ate human flesh; where ape-like people put rings through their noses and swung through trees; where gorilla faced men and women wore only tiny loincloths to cover our bodies as we scurried around in grass huts and spoke unintelligible gibberish. The word "African" and "Savage" became intertwined. "Civilized" came to mean other groups. It means living in a house like other groups, wearing clothes like other people, and being able to speak like other people. To be African was to be dirty, ugly, and subhuman. American born slaves turned away from such identity in disgust, and looked for something else to call themselves, anything other than African (These seven steps were paraphrased from Latif and Latif 1994, *Slavery: The African American Psychic Trauma*).

Blacks lived in what can be referred to as plantation communities or systems. Each plantation was isolated from other plantations and a community of its own. There was almost no communication or travel by slaves between plantations. The distance between plantations was great, and the terrain was barely navigable. We were kept isolated; needed a special pass or permit to travel alone between plantations. Slaves also did not have free access to move around within cities and towns. It was also against the law for a group of slaves to assemble for any purpose without the slave master being in their presence. This would prevent unification, insurrections, or rebellions. Blacks were completely dependent on the master in every way and had no wherewithal of our own.

We could not be fathers to our children or protectors to our women. Slave men were used as stud and mainly kept on the move from plantation to plantation. Sometimes children and/or parents were separated from each other, with little or no regard for family attachments. The family structure was weak, marriages were illegal, and there were no laws to protect the sanctity of slave marriages (Feldstein, 1971, *Once a Slave*; Blassingame, 1973, *Black New Orleans*). A slave marriage required only the consent of the master (Billingsley, 1968, *Black Families in White America*; Rawick, 1972, *The American Slave: A Composite Autobiography*). In some cases, slaves were encouraged to marry, for marriage was to the master like animal breeding, and had as its purpose the increase of his stock (Feldstein, 1971, *Once a Slave*). The slave could have more than one mate, as many as the owner would allow. The master's consent was all that was needed to dissolve a marriage. The master chose the slave's spouse according to qualities which might produce a strong slave offspring to work the fields. Women and men were forced to mate with no regard for emotional attachment. Often children were bred strictly for the auction. Sometimes slaves were beaten severely for minor infractions of the master's rules. The slave was subject only to "plantation law," and not city, county, state or federal law (Feldstein, 1971, *Once a Slave*).

Slaves were separated and not allowed to develop a concept of family in most cases. Blacks were separated at will with no regard for relational ties. There were very few intact Black families. Slavery separated fathers, mothers, and children; slavery helped Blacks to lose what concept of family unity that remained. Black men and women, in most cases, weren't allowed to marry, and were systematically discouraged from forming permanent relationships. The father was not recognized as a factor in his so-called family; even if one was formed. Men and women were both simply recognized as property—to be bought, sold, and used for the whimsical desire of the slave master. This led to a lack of permanent relationships being formed between Black men and women, and later to Black men being quick to leave the family, and having difficulty forming long-lasting marital bonds. Even the mother had very little authority over her children. It has been stated that some slave masters had plantations designed strictly for breeding slaves. Some slave masters would mate a strong, healthy "buck" with a strong, healthy female to produce an offspring that might be strong and healthy for work in the fields.

The slave master ensured that the Black man wouldn't be able to maintain his dignity and self-respect because of the slave master's treatment. The slave could not defend, protect, or be responsible for his family. The slave master could have sex with the slave's woman or abuse his woman or children—both physically and mentally. The slaves were incapable of defending their young daughters from assault. Many of them were raped by the slave master. Many Blacks remain estranged today as a result of their historical experiences. A devastating impression was left on the author after reading Eldridge Cleaver's (1968) *Soul on Ice.* He discussed how the Black woman would call to her man while being misused by the slave master, but the Black man was afraid to answer or defend his woman for fear of his own life. It left the author irate to think how destructive it must have been for the Black man's self-esteem, not to be able to exercise the same territorial prerogative that even lower animals in the animal kingdom are able to exercise: to defend and protect the family. The slave master could go out to the slave's cabin, have sex with his woman, and there was nothing the slave could do. It's my understanding that in some cases the slave would be forced to watch such activities. It was difficult to maintain families, since slaves were considered property and could be sold at any time.

Neither men nor women had the authority to make decisions concerning the family. Blacks learned to depreciate family life and family relationships, their families were broken up, and Black men were used as studs and sent from plantation to plantation. Slaves were even forced to have sex with each other for the purpose of producing babies, who were then snatched away and sold.

Children were used in many cases for whatever the master

desired. Children were frequently separated from parents. Children learned to live in fear of the slave master; and grew up being taught they came from a people who were ugly, stupid, and commanded by God to live as servants. These children were then raped by the slave master, and forced to give birth to his babies, then told that the offspring from these rapes were superior because the children resembled the slave master. Children who were conceived by rape were then taught that the only way he or she will be treated with any kind of respect is if he or she is able to look, speak, and act like the slave master.

Black men learned to see their women as objects and to use for sex only. It was all slaves could do. Women saw men for a similar purpose. Those Black families that did exist were considered temporary, for any member could be sold away at a moment's notice. This destroyed any idea of unifying as a people or family. If a family can't unify there'll be no coming together as a group or race to build better societies or communities (Kardiner and Ovesey, 1962, *The Mark of Oppression*). To have organized societies it is necessary to have basic organization in the family. One's sense of organization usually begins in the family.

This situation left the Black female with a negative impression of the Black male: one that says he wasn't responsible and couldn't protect and defend her or the children. It is felt that even today the Black female has unconsciously passed on to her offspring from generation to generation, a kind of disrespect for the Black male, because of this experience. In the same vain the Black male has passed on disrespect for the Black female. Black females don't respect Black males. Our relationships over a period of time have taken a heavy blow causing there to be little respect in the Black family. Even children don't respect parents. The position the Black male took contributed to his ability to survive during slavery. In this culture we believe that a man should be self-respecting, in control of the situation, responsible, and self-directing—within limitations.

He should also stand up for his rights—regardless. Those things are considered the foundation of his manhood.

The system of slavery dismantled the very cultural foundation of marriage for African Americans. On the plantation, the union between a Black man and woman was more of an economic benefit for the slave master rather than a means of strengthening family ties. Children from such a union represented increase wealth for the master not for the parents. A slave owned no property, and all food and clothing were provided by the master. Slaves not only could not choose our own mates but had little say in rearing of our own children. Slavery destroyed the sense of permanency of marriage, and removed the social training which prepared a young man and woman for the role of spouse. This situation has caused the male to become a stud, and to not feel comfortable in a marital role. Partially as a result, more and more children are being raised by one parent today—usually the mother.

The practice of slave breeding often prevented Blacks from creating permanent relationships. Men and women were matched together for the purpose of producing offspring for the market. Once the woman became pregnant, the man would then be assigned to another female, to impregnate her also. Slavery removed the sacredness of the sex act altogether. The Black woman suffered demoralization. She could be violated with impunity by any man. Under slave law a Black woman's body had no sacred value. Slavery forced sexual immorality. Blacks learned a sense of irresponsibility toward marriage and childbirth. The breakdown in morals between Black men and women has been passed on from generation to generation. Some Black families, economically unstable since slavery, have become second and third generation single-parent welfare dependents. For African Americans the rise of female-headed households is rooted in the condition of male powerlessness introduced during slavery.

Slavery as an American institution was aimed at destroying African traditions and our strong family ties. Under slavery the

Black male was powerless. He could not protect his family, and thereby lost his role as protector of his wife and children. As Bennett, (1969) suggests in *Before the Mayflower*, fatherhood, under this system was a monstrous joke; fatherhood, in fact, was virtually abolished. Slave masters sometimes made the husband subject to the wife. The husband, for example, lived in "Dinah's" cabin and he was "Dinah's Tom."

Again, Bennett (1969) suggests in *Before the Mayflower*, that a Mississippi court ruled that there was no such legal thing as the rape of a slave woman, even after the Emancipation Proclamation. Under protection of the law, other groups raped and beat Black women, and sometimes killed the Black men who protested such actions. In slavery there was no commitment to slave marriages. There was irresponsibility for children and disrespect for the sex act itself.

Since a Black man had no claim to his children, the father of a slave was unimportant. If his wife became pregnant, the child was master's property and could be sold away at the master's whim. Fatherhood, in effect, was outlawed. Slave women learned, after witnessing repeated beatings and lynches of the men, that the men were powerless. Women trained their sons to be submissive to protect them from floggings. Slave women constantly warned the men against making the master angry. In a sense, women became the protector of the family, repressing anger and aggression of the men in their lives as a means of protecting from punishment and even death. In the *Slave Community 1972*, Blassingame observes, "Often a slave would drown himself in a whiskey bottle. If not that he might beat up, stab, or even kill one of his fellow slaves." Whatever the slave said, he rarely carried out his threats. In the eyes of the Black woman, the slave system had made him powerless and weak. Today a Black man will frequently turn to the whiskey bottle or take his frustrations out on a less threatening object.

Blacks came to this country against our will. We came to do the difficult work of an underdeveloped land (Wilhelm, 1970, *Who*

Needs the Negro?). We were meant to serve as inexpensive labor. In slavery Blacks were conditioned away from intellectual pursuits. It was never meant we should be properly educated. The fact remains after almost 400 years that we have never been properly educated. It would be counterproductive for an oppressor to properly educate those whom he oppresses, because it would negate the reason for the oppression. One of the most defined attitudes during slavery and one that persisted throughout the history of this country is, "To educate a slave makes him or her unfit to be a slave." The slave master felt that when you educated slaves you caused them to want to improve conditions. The slave master never wanted this to happen. Freedom, independence, and education are the direct antithesis of slavery.

No educated man or woman would desire a continual existence in slavery. Slave masters believed that it was most beneficial for masters to keep slaves from getting an education. They felt that educating slaves would contribute to the destruction of the slave system. Once slaves were educated, we no longer would desire to be slaves and would seek to overthrow the slave system. It's natural for an educated man to seek justice, liberty, and equality. If adults were fortunate to get some education during slavery, we did so without the slave master's knowledge. From 1619 to 1863, Blacks were conditioned to be slaves. It was against the law to teach a slave to read or write; if slave masters caught slaves attempting to learn to read, they would threaten, beat, maim or kill us. Their objective was definitely to condition the slave to servitude and keep the slaves from getting even a minimal education. In spite of this situation, some slave masters and slave mistresses did teach their slaves to read. And these slaves that learned to read taught other slaves. The slave couldn't fully develop socially, economically, politically, or educationally.

Slavery put the finishing touches on the degradation and dehumanization process. Some social scientists say that slavery scarred and marred Black Americans, and was the most defining experience in America for Blacks. The activities slaves engaged in were designed to condition us to be slaves; we were socially conditioned and bred for slavery. Slavery had the greatest effect on disunity in Black families in America. We are still experiencing the effects from this situation. There came a time when slavery was no longer acceptable, and slaves were supposedly freed with nothing but the clothes on our backs.

It's apparent that much psychological, economic, educational, social, and cultural damage was done to Black Americans as a result of the institution of slavery. It's becoming increasingly apparent that this damage will be a long time in correcting itself if left to its own inertia. Other groups have been very reluctant to atone or provide redress for the situation that occurred. It can be said without a doubt that many of the conditions in the Black community are a direct result of the conditions that existed during slavery. These conditions have been perpetuated from one generation to another over many generations.

On a hot summer evening in the early 1700s, as a slave master was beating his slave because he decided to come in from the fields after a hard day's work, prior to the allotted quitting time, one fellow slave master said to another, "We must never let them overcome their broken state."

If a people are subdued, removed from their environment and left totally dependent, their freedom taken away, their language and culture taken away, their development limited, their education limited, prevented from obtaining employment or capital to take care of their family's needs, their concept of religion distorted—you have thereby disfranchised those people. If given no relief over a period of time, it's only a matter of time before beginning to destroy themselves. There comes a time when outside forces no longer have to further interfere; destruction from the inside becomes automatic.

We were also conditioned to hate ourselves, and everything that looked like us; causing us to feel inferior about whom we were, our skin color, and the rest of our physical characteristics; this caused it to be difficult for us to love one another, have loyalty for one another, to unify, and to eventually consolidate resources. Because we then didn't like ourselves it was difficult to unite; we felt a sense of alienation from one another. This is a part of the overall sense of confusion and disorganization intended as a result of the slave master's efforts to be sure slaves would never develop sufficiently to overcome our situation. As long as families were fractured, men used as studs and sent from plantation to plantation, women used as concubines; there could be no development of love, loyalty, or unity among the slaves. Men who were sent from plantation to plantation could not develop a sense of responsibility for family. Again, this prevented slaves from developing the unity and power to challenge the system. The Willie Lynch letter suggests that the slave master figured out how to disorganize, create distrust, envy, and confuse Blacks for generations to come by magnifying differences and setting us against one another.

Slaves were to have trust for no one but the slave master. In this way, Blacks didn't need to be controlled because we would control ourselves. This was deliberate and has worked to the present day. Slaves were running away, there were uprisings, crops were being left in the fields too long for profit, there were occasional fires, animals were being killed, slaves were becoming obstreperous, injuring ourselves and otherwise out of control. This was occurring to such a great degree that the slave owners invited a man named Willie Lynch from the British West Indies to teach his methods of slave control to the colony of Virginia in 1712. Lynch was a British slave owner in the West Indies. Lynch delivered his speech on the bank of the James River.

He said the idea is to take the differences among the slaves and magnify them. The basis of his control was fear, distrust, and envy. Put the old against the young; light against the dark; intelligent against the less intelligent; large against the small in statue; male against female; have those with fine hair against those with coarse hair; or the tall against the short. In this way use small plantations against larger plantations; attitude of owners against each other; whether the slave lives in the valley, on a hill, east, west, north, south. He said that distrust is stronger than trust, and envy stronger than adulation, respect, or admiration. After being indoctrinated the slave shall carry on and will become self-refueling and self-regenerating for hundreds of years, maybe thousands. You must also have white overseers distrust all Blacks. But it is necessary that your slave trust and depend on only the slave owner. They must love, respect, and trust only the slave owner. In this system the slaves would remain distrustful of one another. This system has worked for hundreds of years; and the black family has remained chaotic, confused, and disorganized—as well as distrustful of one another. The slave owner spent a great deal of time studying and analyzing his slaves. The slave was his property and his living; he wanted to understand how to make best use of this property.

We can overcome this situation and change our present collision course, but we must become consciously and unconsciously aware of our past and present conditioning, and make efforts to recondition ourselves. Slave owners probably never expected slaves to ever become free; therefore, every effort was made to condition them toward a permanent state of servitude.

In order for individuals to be free, they can't simply be told they are free, but must internalize the concept of freedom. It's not enough simply to be removed from the shackles and chains but must be free in one's mind. The Emancipation Proclamation took the chains off the hands, necks, and feet of Black Americans; but did not sufficiently improve our ability to be free mentally. It is important to achieve freedom psychologically before achieving it physically. It is a prerequisite to be free in one's mind before one can completely remove the chains from one's feet. Black Americans did this in reverse. This has resulted in a process by which the minds of Black Americans remain in psychological bondage. Freedom cannot be given it must be taken, says Douglass (1855) in *My Bondage and My*

Freedom, and Clarke (1991) in *Notes for an African World Revolution: Africans at the Crossroads*. Since Black Americans did not develop the wherewithal to take our freedom, we have never been given proper respect as a people. Therefore, since slavery Blacks have never been politically enfranchised and able to develop the power to achieve political, social, psychological, and economic liberation.

Before the end of slavery, our families had been sold from plantation to plantation without any resemblance to a functional family unit, and divided at the will of the slave master. In 1863 Blacks were freed without a clue as to where the rest of our family members were located; if indeed we had any that we were aware of. Some had only a vague notion of where some family members might be. Many men and women left slavery walking with little more than the clothing on our backs. Many were freed with no property, belongings, or wherewithal. Some freedmen walked clear across country until we found family members. Most had to make a new beginning without family, friends, or hope for a brighter future. Some freedmen were successful in finding our long-lost family members, but for some of us, this process only served to further scatter the freedman across the landscape. We then lost what little continuity we had gained in slavery.

The Post-Traumatic Slave Syndrome has been passed down from generation to generation. Many African Americans suffer from the Post-Traumatic Slave Syndrome, regardless of the sex, occupation, or religion. Very few managed to escape the effects, because society continues to reinforce the trauma.

Blacks were conditioned in many ways in slavery: self-hate, dependence, lack of group consciousness, and lack of unity, love, and loyalty. In slavery Blacks were also conditioned toward total impotence: physically, socially, educationally, politically, and psychologically. We had no control over self, family, or the environment. The slave master had complete autonomy over what occurred on his plantation. And again, local, county, state, and federal laws did not apply to the slaves' welfare.

4

───────── ⚮ ─────────

Post-Slavery's Contribution to My Family's Dysfunction

Slavery disconnected the slaves from our culture and heritage. Once slavery had ended, we had no economic, political, social, or educational base from which to begin; this caused us to be severely hampered in our attempt to function as other Americans. This situation only furthered the Post-Traumatic Slave Syndrome. Every attempt was made to frustrate the newly-freed slave's ability to gain true equality.

After slavery, beatings, murder, and psychological abuse was still a fact of life. Other groups wanted to continue to have control of Blacks. So, they reestablished something called Black Codes in 1865, designed to control the movement and activities of the former slaves. The codes were worded differently by different states, but they all were meant to achieve similar results—almost every activity of former slaves was restricted. The former slave had to work for whatever wage was set up by the state and the plantation owners and thought to be fair. If considered vagrant, a Black man could be arrested, and placed on a chain gang (Degruy, 2005, *Post Traumatic Slave Syndrome: America's Legacy of Enduring Injury and Healing*).

These Black Codes also determined what work a Black man could be assigned, where we could do it, and what hours. Black Codes prevented Blacks from purchasing land, voting, suing, or sitting on juries. Frequently the codes established where and with whom we could travel. The Federal courts finally overturned the codes. At that point, another way was figured of how to prevent Blacks from prospering. Some states developed exclusionary laws, restricting the number of Blacks allowed to stay in their jurisdiction.

Blacks were treated after slavery in much the same way as before the end of slavery. Lynches and other types of deaths were frequent with no accountability. Many of the deaths of Black American men, supposedly the results of inappropriate behavior toward other women, but in most cases the allegations were proved false. Some of the behavior we were lynched for was as insignificant as a slight glance (reckless eyeballing). The courts pretended to prosecute some of the other groups for their actions against Blacks, but for the most part, made a mockery of the judicial process. We continued to be treated as slaves and as second-class citizens.

We were segregated and Jim Crowed, discriminated against, and disfranchised through the 1950s and beyond. Jim Crow was a period of separate but equal. We were separate and never quite equal. This turned into outright discrimination that kept Black Americans from entering and being served at public and private institutions, places of amusement, recreational facilities, and even places of worship. There were laws making interracial marriages illegal. Blacks were totally disfranchised. Groups such as the Ku Klux Klan were set up to keep Blacks in line. They beat, exiled, maimed, and killed Blacks: by lynching, drowning, shooting, stabbing, or burning. Black men were killed for the slightest infraction of rules. Neither judge nor jury was necessary (Degruy, 2005, *Post Traumatic Slave Syndrome: America's Legacy of Enduring Injury and Healing*).

From 1866 to 1955, a large number of African Americans had been lynched, many others had been killed by other means, and unreported numbers of women brutalized and raped. Many received beatings at the hands of other groups; in some cases, the police did the beatings, so we can see that slavery did not end traumatic incidents for Black Americans (Degruy, 2005, *Post Traumatic Slave Syndrome: America's Legacy of Enduring Injury and Healing*).

We were never given an opportunity to gain a foothold in the nation's social, economic, political, or educational system. Our ability to travel continued to be limited and tight controls extended. Black Codes became law to curtail the freedom of the newly freed. In no way was there liberty, justice, or equality for Blacks. We were denied an education and opportunities for employment. Blacks continued to have no rights that other groups needed to respect. Blacks were never allowed to develop the ability to improve our lives. Blacks were still dependent on the landowner. Most Blacks became sharecroppers: this meant we worked on the landowner's place for a share of the crop. Most didn't own a house or land, so the landowner allowed us to live on his land and farm it.

Many Blacks had nowhere to go except the plantation, so we stayed under a new arrangement, and sharecropped the land. The sharecropper would give the landowner a certain portion of the crop depending on the arrangement. "The sharecropper did all the cropping, and the landowner did all the sharing of the crop," says James Evans from the popular TV series "Good Times." At harvest time the sharecropper would most often owe the landowner, no matter how hard the sharecropper worked or how rich the soil. The landowner made sure of this. One of the problems was the sharecropper would get supplies from the landowner, and the landowner could tell the sharecropper he owed any amount he wanted. Since the sharecropper's education was usually limited, the landowner could tell him anything he wanted. The landowner charged the sharecropper for what he had received, also for what he didn't receive, and charged it against his crop. When the sharecropper harvested his crop, the landowner would tell him that his crop wasn't enough to get him out of debt. The sharecropper at that point owed the landowner money and was in no position to argue— even if he had an adequate education—which was usually not the case. Arguing would only get him punished severely or killed; even though he was supposedly a free man. Some sharecroppers never got out of debt. Each year the sharecropper was told the same thing that he owed the landowner. The sharecropper usually only got deeper and deeper in debt. The situation obligated the sharecropper to remain on the land to continue working off the debt.

The peonage laws, which lasted in some places until the middle of the twentieth century, would put a sharecropper or worker in jail for leaving if he supposedly owed the landowner.

This was an illegal forcing of Blacks into slavery through debt servitude. Another arrangement was for some Black families having no resources to borrow seeds, tools, mules and supplies needed from local merchants on credit. Some merchants would charge especially high interest rates, where it was next to impossible for the families to ever get out of debt. Some merchants would use the local sharecropper's illiteracy against him, by creative bookkeeping. In any case, when all was said and done, the Black family would find itself in debt to merchants, and would then be cajoled to remain on the farm to work and clear his debt. The next year the sharecropper would find himself in the same situation, and so every year their debt would get larger; thus, the family found themselves in slavery again. Too frequently, this went on for years. It the sharecropper attempted to resist or escape the treatment he would be jailed or fined. If the sharecropper left the landowner would hunt him down and place him in jail. The only way to get away was to slip away in the middle of the night; even then it was hard to keep from getting caught (Degruy, 2005, *Post Traumatic Slave Syndrome: America's Legacy of Enduring Injury and Healing*).

The Convict Lease System was a loophole that developed after slavery and resulted in the continuation of slavery as punishment for crimes. The Black Codes were ruled illegal. Southern plantation owners once again found themselves without inexpensive labor. At the same time Southern states were wondering what to do with former slaves that had committed crimes. Prisons were expensive to build and maintain, and state coffers were all but defunct. The answer, rather than imprison the free Blacks convicted of crimes, was to lease us to former slave owners, as well as proprietors of other businesses, for the remaining of their sentence. This was a win-win situation for the state, business owners, and plantation owners: businesses got cheap labor, the state got paid, and the plantation owner got paid, as well as cheap labor (Degruy, 2005, *Post Traumatic Slave Syndrome: America's Legacy of Enduring Injury and Healing*). Everyone won but the newly freed slave.

It was hard, backbreaking, and manual labor. Convicts were starved, beaten, and brutalized, sometimes sodomized. In some situations, they were worked to death in some of the poorest conditions. We worked in fields, on railroads, and in mines. If one died, the operator of the business would simply ask for a replacement from the state. This life was no better than the life of a slave, at times even worse than that of a slave. None of it mattered, because we were considered less than human, we were branded as criminal (Degruy, 2005, *Post Traumatic Slave Syndrome: America's Legacy of Enduring Injury and Healing*).

In too many situations the charges were false, contrived as a means of legally getting large numbers of inexpensive human laborers. Reckless eyeballing a woman from another race could get you arrested for sexual assault. Refusing to yield to other groups on the sidewalk, or walking on the wrong side of the street might be called disturbing the peace. Not only were many Blacks falsely accused and arrested, but were punished at a much higher rate, and got much longer sentences than other groups. Many others in the South were not ready to give up on slavery. But the whole system of

Convict Lease was rapidly replaced by chain gangs; a similar form of forced labor even more brutal than Convict Lease. The Chain Gang continued until the 1950s. Wealth continued to be built on the backs of Blacks for almost 100 years after the Emancipation Proclamation on what amounted to a slave workforce (Degruy, 2005, *Post Traumatic Slave Syndrome: America's Legacy of Enduring Injury and Healing*).

If one was not looking at the larger picture; life could be quite idyllic, simple, and fulfilling. That is, if one was not ambitious, full of dreams, and worldly-wise; one could make a harmonious adjustment to the environment and situation. A simple life, but such an existence could be pleasant in some ways, even though it was a struggle—without many of life's extras.

Shortly after slavery and the Civil War, between 1865 and 1877, both the South and the North were trying to rebuild. The North was ahead of the South in industrializing, because it had always been that way. Since much of the war was fought in the South, a great deal of the South and its industry had been destroyed. Southern Democrats were still angry because of the destruction that took place there and their subsequent defeat. Nevertheless, the U.S. sought to rebuild the South physically, politically, socially, and economically. There was an attempt by the Republicans to treat Blacks fairly. Blacks were given some high-level political offices, and other government jobs. The Ku Klux Klan became active to counteract the efforts of Republicans. Reconstruction did help many Blacks to progress. It brought on a number of positive social and political changes for Blacks. There was Reconstruction in government, the courts, educationally, and socially: the Fourteenth and Fifteenth Amendments were passed, and many laws and acts were passed with the intent to help the newly freed slaves. State funding for public education began, churches were founded, some Blacks were given land, and a fairer tax system was developed. Southern Democrats soon became discontented with the progress of Blacks. With the help of President Andrew Johnson, the Southern Democrats soon came back into power and began to disfranchise Blacks once again. They slowly began to take control of the government, and by 1877 were in full control. With the help of the Ku Klux Klan and some other groups, Blacks were soon once again completely disfranchised. This discontinued the process of Reconstruction. Reconstruction had done a lot of good for Blacks, but it didn't last long.

It was nineteen years after the end of Reconstruction. Things had returned to normal. Republicans had failed to greatly improve things for blacks. Southern Democrats had returned to power. Jim Crow laws were in full effect. In 1896, *Plessy v. Ferguson* ensured that things would not become equal. Homer Plessy refused to leave his seat on a New Orleans train in 1892, and set in motion a battle that traveled all the way to the United States Supreme Court. The court's 1896 decision permitted states to institute racially separate public accommodations despite the Fourteenth Amendment, which guaranteed all citizens equal protections under the law. It ruled that facilities could be separate and yet equal, but many saw the ludicrousness of this possibility. Many Blacks moved away from the South after slavery, but the big migration push didn't come until much later. Blacks began moving shortly after World War I to large Northern, Western, Eastern and Midwestern cities. Blacks moved to these larger cities to improve their lives.

After 1865, some Black communities were able to get a one-room schoolhouse, outdated books, equipment, and supplies; and access to an inferior education that was made legal in 1896 with the idea of separate but equal in the *Plessy v. Ferguson* case. Separate but equal was the order of the day until *Brown v. Board* in 1954. Many didn't have access to any education, but others were able to get some education even though it was probably inadequate. Some Black children didn't go to school because we lived too far from a school; others had to walk for many miles, sometimes passing a school set aside for other children on the way. Black schools were few. Of those Black communities that had schools, if you wanted to go to a high school, it was a long walk into a larger city. Even some rural-elementary schools were many miles from the child's home. Many Black communities didn't have schools beyond elementary grades. This one-room schoolhouse most Black children attended was usually cold in winter and hot in summer. Supplies and materials were usually inadequate and mostly handed down from other schools in the districts. This remained so for many years. During the early and middle part of the twentieth century, many blacks were still attending that one-room schoolhouse. Many of those who did go to school got time off from school to work the fields. Fieldwork for Blacks took priority over education up to the 1960s in some Southern rural communities. Even during the 1960s some families in the author's small-rural community in East Texas would pick cotton from September through November, before the children began school for the year. The families would give short-term economic gain priority over long-term educational gain.

In the South, many Blacks existed between the 1870s through the 1940s in a shotgun shack with no electricity, gas, or indoor plumbing. Many of my neighbors existed this way, and my parents lived this way until the 1950s. Most of these shacks were heated by a wood-burning fireplace or potbellied stove. This was all the energy they used. Jobs other than sharecropping were hard to find. Most Blacks continued to live on the farm, and on the plantation. Those that moved off the plantation continued to live a marginal existence. Some had dirt roads to their little shack; while others had only a pig trail. A jackleg carpenter built most of the shacks of the period with recycled lumber. Most of the houses were built from lumber taken from a dismantled house or another type of wooden structure. A house was rarely built with new lumber. After the shacks were built, there were no mortgages to pay, and there were no utilities to pay in most cases. We used what was available and that we could afford. Many houses were not built by carpenters but by community people. We grew what we ate and bartered for the rest, we purchased very little from a store: usually spices, flour, cornmeal, or household furnishings, and sometimes household furnishings were homemade. One would trade a bushel of apples for a few chickens. Most of what we used were homemade. We raised animals and grew fruits and vegetables. Not much money changed hands. One was extremely fortunate to have cash. It stayed this way until the great migration when farming began to taper off in the South; and Blacks began to take their chances in larger cities in the Northern, Northeastern, Midwestern, and Western states.

Blacks were conditioned against getting an education—there were too many obstacles. From early history until recently, even if a Black got an education, there were few places to get a job commensurate with that education. The kind of jobs one could get with an education simply weren't available to most Blacks. This conditioned most Blacks to not readily seek an education. If someone tells you, if they see you reading or writing they are going to whip, beat, or cut your hands off; you're likely to shy away from engaging in such activity. You are also likely to unconsciously, if not consciously, pass on to your offspring a dislike for reading—even though your admonishment was only for your own survival. Even if later told that it's okay to read, you are likely to still have some anxieties about doing so. This type of conditioning has been passed on to successive generations of Blacks, to the extent that many still don't value an education. Couple with denied opportunities, discrimination in employment, and inferior schools; it would make for a devastating educational experience that continued into the twenty-first century. The slow progress of Blacks had to do with our coming out of slavery with literally nothing but the clothes on our backs. We were then thrust into a social, economic, and political situation that used every possible tactic to discriminate against us, preventing us from rising above second-class citizenship.

Most Blacks lived in rural areas of the South, but began moving to cities because we were tired of the conditions in the South. With the inventions of the industrial revolution, our labor was no longer necessary—especially in terms of farming. We were conditioned in post slavery the same way we were conditioned during slavery. Blacks simply were not in so-called slavery, but the conditions were basically the same. Blacks had an even harder time making a living during this period. Similar social, economic, political, and educational situations remained. Blacks were conditioned in much the same way as we had been previously. The process has continued until modern times.

Many people would say that slavery ended with the Emancipation Proclamation, but there are some signs that indicate slavery is an ever-present factor in the lives of many Blacks. Even though this is true, many Blacks would deny that we continue to be slaves. Many Blacks live under an illusion that we have freedom and independence, but in fact don't recognize the nature of our condition, and engage in denial about our true situation. Sometimes we just don't realize our condition or the situations that have contributed to our condition. Blacks sometimes confuse being loose from the chains with being free and independent. The "ideal slave" is one who doesn't recognize that he or she is a slave, and will attempt to engage in denial about our status as a slave. The ideal slaves will also minimally resist enslavement, suggests Batu Shakari, a noted Chicago activist. Many groups continue to resist efforts to provide any kind of redress for what happened in slavery, or since slavery—never mind that the sweat and blood of Blacks helped to build this country. It seems that reparations will be a long time coming. We have never benefited from the labor we put into helping to build this country.

John Henrik Clarke, a late and great Black historian said, in one of his public lectures, "Slavery has not been abolished; it has been transformed." Blacks in most cases owe what they earn to those who control the economy, and each time we receive our "legal tender," it's usually never quite enough to rise above our individually accumulated deficits for the month. Blacks must understand that there are justifiable reasons to question whether we've ever been psychologically free in this country. Today many refer to what can be described as a "modern form of slavery," and say that Blacks exist in merely a different form of slavery. Blacks were officially emancipated but many of the conditions never changed. The slave quarters quickly became the modern ghetto. The cotton field was replaced by a regular 9 to 5 job for some individuals.

After emancipation, African American men sought to regain dignity and a sense of manhood, by working hard to provide for our families. Whether this took the form of sharecropping, working on the railroad, or working in Northern factories, we prided ourselves on being able to take care of our families. As other groups sought to relegate Blacks to the lowest paid jobs and thereby maintain other groups' dominance in society, Black couples realized the necessity of working together to make ends meet. Often Black women would get jobs as domestics, or in the case of sharecroppers, would work in the fields along side the husband. Today women are able to find jobs while men are being laid off. Men being out of work cause emotional strain on marriages. If the man was raised in a household where the father was dependent or physically absent, he may feel pressure to leave the household. Also, economic disputes frequently cause a man to leave the household. Fear of being disrespected, disregarded, and ultimately humiliated creates extreme paranoia and insecurity in Black men and women. People who have been taught to feel badly about themselves cannot give praise and encouragement to others, something which is essential to build a healthy relationship.

The slave master not only studied "ideal slave management" but also attempted to apply scientific principles to slave management. This resulted in slaves being well conditioned (Breeden, 1980. *Advice Among Masters: The Ideal Slave Management in the Old South*).

5

☙❧

Modern-Day Contributions to My Family's Dysfunction

Since slavery Black Americans have labored to recover from the dehumanization of bondage, the offense of Peonage, the outrage of the Black Codes, the affront of Convict Leasing, Chain Gangs, the indignities of Jim Crow, and the ravages of poverty. But the Black family has continued to raise its offspring to survive in less than favorable circumstances, many assaults, disrespects, and blocked goals.

Lynches are an anachronism. Black women and young children are rarely physically abused. In most cases we have the right to vote without being obstructed. Some say we have almost leveled the playing field. But race is still a problem in this country. We can't count our chickens just yet. Civil rights legislation come up short in its effort to level the playing field, provide equality, and justice for all.

Presently, to a large extent, the shadow of slavery is still casting

49

a reflection over this land, affecting the daily lives of all African Americans (Clarke, 1991, *Notes for an African World Revolution: Africans at the Crossroads*). "The Black family has not completely recovered because many factors and behaviors from the slavery experience continue today" (William, 1991, p. 4, *They Stole it but You Must Return it*). Black Americans experience many unique disadvantages throughout our lives (Nobles, Goddard, Cavil & George, 1987, *African-American Families: Issues, Insights and Directions*). The centuries of senseless cruelty and the permeation of the Black man's character, economic exploitation, racial oppression, political domination, and disfranchisement are still ever-present realities in the African American's experience. To understand the dynamics which are prevalent in the African America family today, it is necessary to understand the experiences and situations from which these dynamics were initiated. African Americans continue to experience many unique disadvantages throughout their lives (Nobles, Goddard, Cavil & George, 1987, *African-American Families: Issues, Insights, and Directions*). "The centuries of senseless cruelty and the permeation of the black man's character with the conviction of his own hatefulness and inferiority tell a sorry tale" (Grier & Cobbs, 1980, p. 208, *Black Rage*). The lives of African Americans have been painful, desolate, and filled with grief, bitterness, self-hatred, rage and blind hopelessness. The process normally begins with the child, and it is ultimately manifested in the adult.

> The horror carries the endorsement of centuries and the entire lifespan of a nation. It is a way of life which reaches back to the beginnings of recorded time. And all the bestiality, wherever it occurs and however long it has been happening is narrowed, focused, and refined to shine into a black child's eyes when first he views his world. All that has ever happened to black men and women he sees in the victims closest to him, his parents.

A life is an eternity and throughout all that eternity a black child has breathed the foul air of cruelty. He has grown up to find that his spirit was crushed before he knew there was need of it. His ambition, even in their forming, showed him to have set his hand against his son. That is the desolation of black life in America (Grier & Cobbs, 1980, p. 208, *Black Rage*).

Since the so-called demise of slavery, the African American's experience has been filled with many dilemmas. Only now are we beginning to sense the burden placed on African American children by a nation which does not want them to grow into mature men and women (Grier & Cobbs, 1980, *Black Rage*). "Persisting to this day is an attitude, shared by black and other groups alike, that blacks are inferior. This belief permeates every facet of this country and it is the etiological agent from which has developed that national sickness" (1980, p. 31). Through a conscious process transmitted by other groups, an unconscious process transmitted by parents, and daily conditioning and programming, African American children soon learn to hate and despise themselves and those who look like them.

Grier and Cobbs (1980, *Black Rage*) makes the following statements about how African Americans learn to despise themselves:

For black and other groups alike, the air of this nation is profuse with the idea of other groups supremacy and everyone grows to manhood under this influence. Americans find that it is a basic part of their nationhood to despise blacks. No man who breathes this air can avoid it and black men are no exception. They are taught to hate themselves, and if at some point they discover that they are the object of this hatred, they are faced with an additional task, nothing less, for the imperative remains—Blacks are to be despised.

Thus, the dynamics of Black self-hatred are unique. They involve the child's awareness that all people who are Black as he is are so treated by other groups. Whatever hostility he mounts against other groups finds little support in the weakness and the minority status of Black people. As it is hopeless for him to consider righting this wrong by force, he identifies with his oppressor psychologically in an attempt to escape from his hopeless position. From his new psychologically "oppressed" position, he turns on Black people with aggression and hostility and hates Blacks and, among the Blacks himself (pp. 198-199).

Unable to directly release our anger and frustration on the oppressive conditions of ghetto life, Black Americans take out our frustrations and bitterness on ourselves and each other. The psychological forces which turns aggression outward against other Blacks is one of the devastating features of racial and class oppression. Most colonial people display the same pattern of internalized aggression and violence against our own people. Violent acts against other Blacks become an accepted and safe way to vent aggression; it is the "normal" way in which people respond (Hutchinson, 1990, *The Mugging of Black America*). In view of all of the foregoing statements, the Post-Traumatic Slave Syndrome continues, as a result of this programming.

Freud said a person's basic personality is formed by the time he's six years of age. Neo-Freudians have suggested something similar, but also suggest the personality is malleable throughout the lifecycle. If Freud is anywhere near correct, we can at least say the basic personality is formed early in life. We can also say that once we are conditioned, and had that conditioning reinforced on a regular basis, we are set for life.

The past always has a heavy influence on the present. It is difficult to escape past conditioning. But the bigotry, racism, prejudice, and discrimination that exist today is enough to keep Black families struggling to survive. Mostly it is past conditioning that sets the tone for the future. Once conditioning has taken place it is hard for this conditioning to become extinct, especially when it is being reinforced on a daily basis. Things haven't changed all that much, and conditions are reinforced on a moment-to-moment, daily, weekly, and monthly basis.

Black Americans toil under practically the same conditions we always have, and many things really haven't changed. We're treated much the same as always. We got behind a long time ago, and now find it difficult to catch up and keep up. Things have not changed throughout the country. People now have water bills, gas, and telephone bills, as well as mortgages. Most people will for most of their lives pay rents or mortgages on their property. Food is purchased at the store. You can't simply walk out your back door and butcher a hog or cow—too many health considerations. Individuals rarely grow their own food; everything must be bought at exorbitant prices. There are few barters or giveaways. At one time if a neighbor butchered a hog or cow, it would be shared with everyone in the community. Chances are what you didn't grow you could barter from a neighbor. That kind of activity rarely exists any more. This makes life in the city hard for some individuals, and especially for those who are familiar with a different style of existence. Maladjustment forces some people into a life of crime, others simply have difficulty adjusting to the city. Ever since Blacks encountered other groups in Africa we've been disrespected and taken advantage of. It has led to the present situation of Blacks labeled as second-class citizens.

Today Blacks in America still experience a great deal of racism, prejudice, and discrimination; though many things in America have improved for Blacks. Blacks in America have come a long way. The first group of Blacks were noted as coming to this country in 1619. Each generation of Blacks since that time has faced similar systematic discrimination, racism, and prejudice. There was never in the history of the United States been anything more than momentary reprieves in these basic conditions.

It seems apparent that the rights, privileges, and liberties of Blacks have been historically cyclical. The old idea of, *now you have them—now you don't,* have been fully operational. Just when we thought we were making progress, something came along to disrupt our forward movement, and put us into yet another holding pattern. Blacks have only enjoyed brief periods of progress in this country— and then a return to business as usual.

It's believed this has occurred because other groups have been hoping we'd sooner or later destroy ourselves, go back to Africa, or someone in power would devise a way to bring about our ultimate demise without too much fanfare. Several historical figures have proposed sending Blacks back to Africa. But neither of these has happened, and we keep on coming. It is not felt the powers-that-be have given up on one of these events occurring. There are many examples of how Blacks have made progress, only to later be forced into a regressive pattern.

When Blacks first came to this country, we were considered indentured servants in many cases. Many of us had worked our way out of indentured servitude by the 1660s and had purchased land. We were fully integrated with some other groups in many ways. Then the colonists decided they needed total Black slave labor with the increase in tobacco production in the colonies. Blacks were then prevented from owning land or intermarrying and relegated to a more permanent form of servitude.

In the 1790s it seemed as though things would change for the better for Blacks. Blacks were beginning to enjoy greater civil rights. It was soon after the Revolution, the nation was becoming more prosperous, and it was rapidly growing. But with the invention of the cotton gin, a new need for slaves was developed. Thus, there was more of a need to suppress, restrict, control, and to rely on this slave labor to produce the cotton necessary to fuel the economy. This meant reduction in the rights of Blacks.

Near the end of slavery, a few Blacks were buying their freedom, having it given to them, or getting free in other ways. We were making some progress even though it was slow movement toward our complete freedom and independence. But then the Black Codes were legislated and designed to restrict the freedom of those Blacks who were considered free, to curtail our mobility. Throughout the South, free Blacks found our mobility curbed, our economic opportunity limited, and our civil rights all but obliterated.

After slavery, Blacks began to progress with Reconstruction (1865-1877), which made it possible for some Blacks to get government and high political offices. Republicans, who were more favorable toward Blacks at this time, were backing this movement throughout the South. But Reconstruction ended because Southern Democrats thought Blacks were making too much progress, and President Andrew Johnson supported the Democrats. After Reconstruction, Jim Crow laws were established. These policies severely restricted the freedom of Blacks across the country. Democrats regained control in the South, and conditions returned to pre-Reconstruction politics.

Blacks weren't making much progress in 1896, but African Americans still had great hopes and expectations. The country was involved in an industrial revolution, and some historians seem to think animosity toward Blacks was subsiding in some circles. This period produced such men as Booker T. Washington and W. E. B. Du Bois, but *Plessy vs. Ferguson* decided there was nothing wrong with racial separation as long as facilities were equal. This case impeded progress and set race relations back a hundred years or more. These are just a few situations where Blacks' progress has been sent into a tailspin; to recall all of the events would be too numerous.

African Americans have always had the illusion that the next president would make their basic rights more secure, or the next elected official would aid in doing so, when these individuals mostly only maintained the status quo.

After making some progress over the years, with increasing economic and job opportunities; Blacks are once again suddenly moving toward fewer job opportunities, having more difficulty getting on welfare, and increasingly unstable Social Security. In addition, our rights have become more and more like pawns to be manipulated.

If you don't believe the rights of Blacks have been cyclical throughout history, you should closely study the history of Blacks in these United States.

Blacks also are still being conditioned to negativity on a daily basis, and reinforced in similar ways as throughout the past. These days it's subtle. These things cause our behavior to be much the same as always. The society takes every opportunity to deny Blacks equal opportunities, and pretend that things are different now and everybody has equal rights.

Blacks have been discriminated against, for one reason or the other, since the beginning. Blacks have been the victims of every conceivable kind of exploitation, intimidation, violence, murder, fraud, and disfranchisement—to a much greater degree than other ethnic groups. Blacks haven't had the opportunity to adapt, to develop a common bond, or the economic opportunities available to other groups. The denial of these opportunities that were readily available to other ethnics had devastating consequences for Blacks. The local, state, and federal governments have for many years failed to provide protection, employment, and services.

Only Blacks have experienced the devastating complications of attempted genetic suicide; of being stolen from ancestral families and deprived of names, language, culture, legacy, inheritance, family, and religion. Blacks alone have survived the dehumanization of slavery across generations and found themselves segregated and economically dependent in a society unwilling to make restitution for its injustices against us. Blacks alone have been exploited for their labor, creativity, and productivity from generation to generation. No other group can truly claim these experiences.

These conditions have caused many problems in Black families: children to drop out of school at phenomenal rates; we have the highest rate of homicides among our young men; we hurt each other, both physically and mentally; we maim and even kill each other disproportionally; we fail to support each other, and then work against each other; we attempt to destroy ourselves through drugs, alcohol, and destructive relationships at a high rate; we fail to build institutions to ensure the survival of family, community, and culture; we fail to build institutions for the training and development of the youth; we have suicides; a high rate of teen pregnancies; a high rate of AIDS/HIV; we have drive-by shootings and other homicides; mental illness; child abuse and neglect; imprisonment; incredible amounts of single-parent families; family disruption, disintegration, and many other family problems; and other negative conditions. In addition, we've failed to adjust to an ever-changing, technological-progressive society, which is one reason why we continue to have a high rate of unemployment.

Part of the problem with Blacks is our education has been designed to make us hate ourselves, and to have respect for other groups but none for our own group. Education in America has historically meant indoctrination into other groups' culture. Images of other groups are constantly put before us. Blacks are told that we haven't contributed anything worthwhile to civilization. An "educated" person is one who is well versed in other groups history, literature and philosophy.

There is no equal opportunity in education. Dropout rates in inner-city schools are as high as 60%. These schools in urban areas are overcrowded and devoid of resources, while suburban schools are flourishing. Unemployment among African Americans is twice as high as for other groups. Blacks earn approximately 75% of the level for other groups, regardless of the level of education.

Blacks have many problems in their families. A large percentage of our families are headed by a single female. The dating ritual often leads to physical intimacy, but not marriage. Relationships frequently don't last for a long period of time. Women often feel bitter and cheated. There is little respect for the institution of marriage. We have experienced tremendous growth in the prison population. At this point Blacks consist of too large a percentage of the prison population, when we are only a small percentage of the total United States population. We continue to get unfair treatment from the police. Some Blacks find it difficult to qualify for a loan from banks. Blacks are still disfranchised in many respects. The 2000 election in Florida demonstrated how we are still disfranchised. Four-hundred years of physical, psychological, educational, and spiritual disfranchisement have left a mark.

The principles the slave master applied were so effective that the efficacy of principles of "ideal slave management" (Breeden, 1980, *Advice Among Masters: The Ideal Slave Management in the Old South*) is still apparent in the behavior of Blacks today. Even today some parents discourage their children from reading, because it is said that book learning has no value; it is for sissies—just use common sense. This is nothing more than a conditioned attitude that had its origins in slavery.

Today Blacks rarely support one another. Our conditioning is such that even if another Black person has a business, we'd rather call someone else. In some cases, we've been conditioned to believe that the Black person will not provide the same level of service. This fact keeps money from circulating within our communities. It also keeps our communities from growing and developing (Kunjufu, 1991, *Black Economics*).

When my parents first got married there was only a three-mile trail leading off the main road in 1929. There was only a trail that winded its way pass the several houses on the trail. There were tree limbs, creeks, and deep ditches along this trail. It was impossible to traverse this trail in anything but a wagon, on feet, or on horseback. Some of the ditches were deep enough to almost hide a house. At the wrong time this trail would become difficult to negotiate: when it rained the trail would become impossible; at other times the mud, dew, and tree limbs would become obstacles. But my parents managed to transport the materials on a wagon and build the house. It is hard to imagine how this was done by wagon. When my older sisters and brothers were children, family members walked to the bus stop at the end of this three-mile pig trail. Family members walked through the mud, the dew, the streams, the grass, the ditches, and the overhanging-tree limbs. I'm sure that not having a decent road contributed to siblings dropping out of high school and leaving home prematurely. The family was isolated from all but the most determined traveler. My oldest sisters and brothers walked several miles to a little community school. When the youngest children got older, siblings transferred to a school further north in Homer, Louisiana proper.

Each family did its part to cut weeds, remove the fallen-tree limbs, and whatever else needed to be done. In the early part of my childhood I remember helping to cut weeds from, and to patch up the trail. Before the graded road was constructed my relatives confined travel to daytime. There were always stories about wild men, wild animals, ghost, and goblins along the trail. Along with these things simply navigating the trail could be physically dangerous.

My sisters, brothers, and parents found the trail difficult to contend with. But the trail was a consistent factor in our lives. We did all our traveling by negotiating one trail or another. But most of my siblings soon got tired of these trails and moved to larger cities. My brothers simply left and moved to the Gulf Coast. My sisters got married and moved to cities not far away. It is not too farfetched to assume that leaving the farm was hastened by the situation we lived in. After a while my father moved to the Gulf Coast and found a job. It was too difficult for family members trying to negotiate this trail on their way to a job in the city.

The whole community in those days was connected by a series of trails. Though, the automobile by this time had been invented a number of years ago, most folks still traveled by wagon and horseback. This was a backward community. Everything was within walking distance. There was a general store and a school. People bartered with each other for commodities. There were people in the community with at least some rudimentary skills. People didn't have to go outside the community to get things done. There were carpenters, blacksmiths, bricklayers, though most of the houses were constructed of wood. Most of the houses did have a chimney or fireplace. People built their own houses, butchered their own animals, grew their own food, repaired their own tools, built their own fences, and served as midwives for their own children. Most took care of their own animals. It was a self-contained, independent, and self-sufficient community. People lived a simple lifestyle. Medical needs were cared for by someone who specialized in home remedies. Some individuals specialized in the treatment of sick animals. Though the automobile had been invented for a few years, there were no automobiles before the road was constructed. I have no idea why the county didn't begin to build a road earlier—possibly because of discrimination, it's the only explanation I can think of. The idea was to do as less as possible for a disfranchised, non-voting, and invisible-minority population. It could be more complicated than that. Town was at least twenty miles away, and the only way to get there was on horseback or wagon. Sometimes my father and community people would ride a horse to town on Saturday mornings. We lived isolated lives as if we were eighteenth century prairie farmers. At one time my folks didn't even buy groceries from the store like some people did. The only things purchased from a store were salt, flower, cornmeal, sugar, and other spices. Everything else was purchased, grown, or bartered for in the community. If you grew apples and another man grew chickens, you could barter some chickens for a bushel of apples.

A man even specialized in building furniture, though it might have been crude.

My parents had ten children. There are several theories why older parents had so many children. One is that women simply had a child every so often to correspond with their monthly cycle until menopause. Another is that most people were rural farmers and wanted to have children to work the farm for as long as possible, and perhaps someone to take care of them in their old age. That's the way they did it in many countries. But some parents certainly had more children than others. Before 1935 there was no such thing as Social Security. My parents were born at the very beginning of the twentieth century. There were at least ten children in most of the families in my community. One family was noted as having twenty-two children, of course the children were by different women.

I'm not sure why my parents decided to have ten children. I figure it was a combination of these reasons, along with the fact that if there was such a thing as birth control in those days, my parents did not have any access to them. My mother didn't exactly keep up with modern methods of living, as most women in the community didn't at that time. I don't think my mother ever changed her basic approach to life from what she learned in her childhood; even though many major changes took place in the earlier and latter part of the twentieth century. The automobile, the airplane, refrigeration, and air conditioning were all developed during the early and latter years of her life. In fact, most modern developments occurred during this period. Part of the reason she never changed her approach to life was because of her general isolation.

There were no community organizations or institutions in my community. There was no community center, playgrounds, Little League, Pewee football, or basketball leagues. Blacks didn't vote—which contributed to their disfranchisement. No organizations to promote the growth and development of the community. There was only drinking, philandering, and gambling. All this made for a dysfunctional family and community. We considered ourselves lucky to have food to eat, a few clothes to wear, and a roof over our heads—even if it did leak when it rained.

The church wasn't a major factor in our community, but at least we had a building. My first remembrance of attending church was when I was approximately eleven-years old. I would drive an old Black 1951 Fleetline standard-shift Chevrolet to take my mother to church. My brother John had left home and left behind that old Chevrolet. It was parked in a deteriorated garage sitting next to the house. He had taught me how to drive it before he left for the Gulf Coast. I could barely see out the windshield. Prior to having a car to drive my mother would walk through the woods, the pastures, and the fields, to get to church. Neither of us liked walking across the fields because the ticks were numerous in the tall grass.

The church sat near the end of a red-dirt road. It had a rusty-tin roof. There was no fan or air conditioner. A potbellied stove heated the church in winter. It had rough-hewn pine seats that would grab and tear you clothing in a hot second. It was always dusty.

Usually a lay minister gave a sermon each Sunday. Sometimes we would get a visiting minister. Only about 2-8 people showed up each Sunday. There was no Sunday school or programs for the youth, because I was the only young person to show up each Sunday.

The people believed in a blue-eyed, blonde-headed Jesus. But if Blacks truly believe in such a Jesus, what does that say about us as a people. To believe in such a Jesus is to believe in one's own inferiority. Every people on Earth see their God in the likeness of themselves, but Blacks' God happen to be in the likeness of other groups. Part of the dysfunction of Black people has to do with us seeing our God in this likeness. Blacks are in a foreign culture and have had to adopt the God of a foreign land. This accounts for part of our confusion, disorganization, and chaos. If we are to ever improve our condition, we must begin to see our God in our own image. It will prove fatal for us to continue to see our God in the image of a people unlike ourselves. Other groups had to see God in their own image; this was in keeping with Blacks as inferior and other groups as superior. If you have to appeal to another group's god to meet your every need, a god in the image of a people who enslaved you, what does that say for your self-esteem? My family members were indoctrinated under these conditions. As Africans, part of our problem is that we have adopted a foreign way of relating to the world. We tend to pattern our relationships from the Bible, when the Bible consist of stories that have been fabricated. In many cases we learned to pattern our relationships after conditioning in slavery. Blacks have never learned to truly cultivate our relationships.

Given the history of Blacks we are lucky to have survived in any condition. Blacks have come a long way. The fact that we have had several Black men run for president speaks for itself. But there's still much discrimination, racism, and prejudice. The main thing affecting Blacks today, even more so than racism, discrimination, and prejudice, is our past. Our past continues to handicap us: conditions have been passed on from generation to generation, creating negative situations for the present. Today, it's true that we do more damage to ourselves than any other groups could possibly do. But it's because of negative conditioning throughout our history.

Few Blacks or anyone else wants to talk about how we got this way. But as a result of conditioning during pre-slavery, slavery, the Middle Passage, post-slavery, and present-day, it has caused us to exhibit certain negative behaviors. This conditioning explains why many Black Americans are confused, chaotic, and disorganized; why we lack love, loyalty, unity, or the ability to consolidate resources. It also explains why we have much self-hate as well as self- and other-destructive behaviors in our families.

It should be realized that many changes have been made in this society regarding its treatment of Black Americans. But it must also be understood that as a society a lot of work needs to be done. You'll find a different set of conditions for blacks; depending on what state and what city you consider. Discrimination, racism, and prejudice aren't uniform between individuals, groups, or nationalities. It's time to become concerned about the general social, economic, political and educational conditions in society.

The society has indeed come a long way from pre-slavery, Middle Passage, slavery, post-slavery: from carrying that greasy bag of fried chicken—prepared by mom or grandma—especially for traveling, because one couldn't get service in restaurants along the way. Blacks also couldn't get a room in most motels and hotels along the highway. Gas stations along the way would sell Blacks gas, but they had to use the colored only bathrooms and water fountains. In some cases, we had to relieve ourselves in the forest along the highway, because some gas stations didn't have a restroom for Blacks. Colored only signs have been removed, and Blacks can eat at restaurants along the interstate. The only problem is too many of us can't afford the price of a meal. Most motels and hotels will gladly give us a room if we can afford it.

This society is a long way from being color-blind. Poor public service is still the norm for Blacks in many areas of society. There are still problems in going certain places, living certain places, and participating in certain activities.

At one time there was no doubt where you stood. You were considered a second-class citizen and you knew it. Today, discrimination is subtle, not as blatant as it used to be. It's also more economic. But many still haven't changed their basic prejudicial attitudes. In many cases discrimination occurs and it seems it's not because of ethnicity. Sometimes it seems it's an issue of class. This still leaves many Blacks disfranchised.

Blacks are getting better employment opportunities but still have a high rate of unemployment. It used to be a time when the only professional jobs available to Blacks were either teaching or preaching—then there were the unskilled or menial jobs. Some of this had to do with poor educational opportunities. Because of the educational system in the Black community we still aren't prepared for many job opportunities.

In addition, too many of the available jobs are out-sourced to other countries. You'll find some Blacks in most type jobs, but few in top-level jobs. There's still the glass-ceiling operating. Society also finds it easier to employ immigrants than give these jobs to Blacks, even in their own community. There's still much racism, prejudice, and discrimination that block Blacks from obtaining employment.

Black have come a long way from the one-room schoolhouse with the potbellied stove. At that time most of their books, supplies, and materials were inadequate. Air in winter came through the cracks in the walls, and it was hot during other periods. Schools were discontinued in the spring so Black children could participate in farming activities. During the regular term in the fall Black children were also excused so we could help with the farm chores (overheard in a conversation between my mother and father).

Blacks are able to get a better education in today's society. Society no longer presents certain of these issues, but Blacks still in some cases have unqualified teachers in certain subjects; and still have inadequate books, supplies, and materials in some cases. In other cases, there are leaky roofs, broken windows, and plaster falling off the walls (a personal observation). This occurs because of inequities in funding for our schools.

Some of the problem is our children still receive poor motivation from home, and teachers have low expectations for children. The past continues to impact the present education of Black children: some negativity gets passed on from generation to generation. Children are constantly bombarded with the quick and easy way to obtain success. Many of them lack motivation to achieve success the old-fashion way, by postponing immediate gratification. There're also too few opportunities for a higher-level education. Blacks continue to have a high-dropout rate in high school, a low enrollment rate in college, and a low-graduation rate from college (some personal observations).

Laws are passed but they have not changed the hearts and minds of the majority of Americans. No matter what level at which some Blacks function, there's still the belief that most Blacks are incapable of performing on a par with the rest of society. The general society still holds many negative stereotypes about Blacks.

More than 150 years after the Emancipation Proclamation and more than 60 years after *Brown vs. Board of Education of Topeka*, segregation remains constant. Issues of race and problems of the color line are still pressuring us, because they continue to be the most persistent problems facing the society. Seldom does understanding exist between Blacks and other groups. On the surface we are cordial with each other, but frequently this intolerance for one another unmasks unresolved issues. Blacks are presented with countless incidents of discrimination, assaults, and other mistreatment directed at them and their love ones (Degruy, 2005, *Post-Traumatic Slave Syndrome: America's Legacy of Enduring Injury and Healing).*

Today, the Post-Traumatic Slave Syndrome as a legacy of slavery and oppression remains etched in our eternal souls. The impact of this Post-Traumatic Slave Syndrome can be observed daily in our struggle to understand who and what we are, and in our unclear vision of whom and what we can become. The effects of this historical situation can be seen in our continuous fight for respect, which we desire and require from without, but that only can be acquired from within. These impacts can be witnessed in the war between affirmative "racial education" in our homes and communities, and destructive "racist education" everywhere else, a war that we seem to be letting slip through our fingers (Degruy, 2005, *Post-Traumatic Slave Syndrome: America's Legacy of Enduring Injury and Healing*).

PART II

My Mother Became Paranoid, My Father Punked Out, and My Family Fell Apart

"Your crisis is God's opportunity to deliver a miracle."
-----Anonymous

"The Almighty God exists in each of our lives."
----Jay Thomas Willis

"God will give you grace for your season."
---Anonymous

"When you are at the bottom ain't no place to go but up."
----Anonymous

"An unprepared mind will self-destruct."
----Anonymous

6

C3◆80

My Own Dysfunction as it Relates to Historical Conditions

My family's dysfunction as well as my own is related to my historical conditions. My parents were only several generations out of slavery and had once been sharecroppers. All my mother knew was the farming way of life. We lived at the end of a three-mile trail that connected to a meandering, hill-ridden, curvaceous, blacktopped, and two-lane highway. A trail led beyond our house to connect with another dirt road running north and south. This part of the trail was rarely traveled. My house sat in what was only a clearing in the forest. This trail to my house was narrow. Because of our isolation there were few visitors. Until I was six-years old we had no electricity, gas, telephone, or indoor plumbing. When the road was constructed it was possible to have electricity, as a freshman in high school butane was obtained, in college telephone service became available, and after I worked for several years, plumbing was made possible.

I was born on October 20, 1947, on a cool-rainy night. My birth was assisted by several midwives from the community. Most Blacks didn't give birth in hospitals because of historical patterns of segregation. It was immediately after World War II and not long after the Depression. The war and the Depression caused my family to experience more lack than would have been ordinarily experienced. It was a bad time for the poor to live and be born. Of course, the war and the Depression didn't have a great effect on most Black families, because of being used to lack of education, lack of employment, and poverty conditions. I was born at this particular place and time to the particular parents for a reason. Only God knows that reason. Apparently, He had something in mind for me.

My mother made me wear my sister's old-hand-me-down dresses until I was three-years old. She didn't seem to think about it one way or the other. It was right after the war and not long after the Depression—commodities were scarce. We made do with the basic necessities of life. My mother kept me in pigtails so I wouldn't have to get a haircut.

We existed on subsistence farming. The land could barely grow anything but the hardiest of weeds. We had cows, horses, dogs, chickens, pigs, guinea fowls, and ducks. We raised cotton, corn, peas, watermelons, cantaloupes, cushaws, squash, okra, sweet potatoes, Irish potatoes, tomatoes, and vegetables of all types. At the time most of what we raised was for our own consumption. My mother canned everything she could. There were peaches, pears, and apple trees. Grapes, plums, and pecans grew wild in the forest. My family would eat chickens, butcher a hog once a year, and occasionally slaughter a cow every now and then.

School was a dysfunctional experience. I started to school at seven years of age. My birthday came in October. I was only five in September, so I had to wait until the next year. That's the way things worked in North Louisiana in 1953.

No one in my family had tried to teach me colors, geometric shapes, the alphabet, or my numbers. I had no toys to play with, and my manual dexterity was grossly underdeveloped. In school no teacher tried to teach me how to form my letters, and even today I form my letters poorly. I was like a plant sitting in the corner.

To top that off, I was handicapped by an outdated, all-Black school that didn't pay me any attention. The school I attended was a small all-Black-rural one. The elementary, junior high, and high school were combined at one location. It was twenty miles away from my home in a town of approximately 5,000. Some days I came to school poorly dressed, because my mother didn't pay much attention to me. In some cases, my hair wasn't combed or brushed. My hygiene was usually poor, since we had no indoor plumbing. Teachers never questioned why I came to school unkempt as I did. I was invisible for all intent and purpose. In addition, I had a severe stuttering habit. When I entered school, the teachers never paid me much attention either. I sat there like a lump on a log—going through the motions; day after day I sat there, taking in what I could. It's a good thing too, for otherwise I probably wouldn't have survived. My speech impediment and my unkempt appearance caused my teachers to handle me with a long-handled spoon. The basics should have been a general practice since teachers knew we didn't get kindergarten or preschool. My handwriting was atrocious. It got better after I got to college and began writing on a regular basis, but my writing was scribble up to that point. No teacher ever said anything about my writing. I had a lot of catching up to do and ended up getting further and further behind. Many of our books were discarded from the other part of the district. We weren't required to read other than the textbooks, and most of us didn't read them.

It was much like the one-room schoolhouse depicted in historical literature, except there was a classroom for each grade. The buildings were cold in winter and hot the rest of the year. Needless to say, we as a school were underfunded, and had just the bare necessities. Black schools have been underfunded for most of their history, causing children to get an inadequate education. Even my school situation came from a historical legacy of slavery. My entire elementary, junior, and high school education was neglected. Before I was aware of what was going on, I had been severely crippled.

I don't remember my education before the fifth grade. I remember in fifth grade we had a fairly good teacher. But she neglected us in order to spend time with her music students. She was the only music teacher for elementary, junior high, and high school. When she would practice her music students for upcoming concerts, she would take the class to the music room with her. The budget for the school was so limited that they didn't want to pay for a music teacher and a fifth-grade teacher.

In sixth grade, I got placed in the band director's class. He taught band and the sixth grade. Again, the district didn't want to pay for a band director and a sixth-grade teacher, so the teacher had to pull double duty. This was a part of our historical legacy of underfunding in our schools. I got a reprieve from class every day in order to go to the band room. I missed out on a lot of valuable class time. Even when we were in class, we did very little that was productive. He was not a good teacher or band director. I joined the band in sixth grade.

The next year I was unfortunate enough to get the same band director for seventh grade. Once we had to do a rare assignment. I picked up a piece of paper from the floor with some writing on it and turned it in to him. He put a mark in his grade book and a mark on my paper. It was the only assignment I remember doing in that year. The band director got a break from class the hour before the noon hour to catch up on band related activities. The rest of my class had a course in Louisiana history, while I went to the band room with the band director. It was amazing that I spent so much time around him, but he never tried to teach me to read a single note of music. Later I found out that Louisiana History was a required course in most Louisiana schools.

In eighth grade things didn't get any better. There were two sections of the class as there had always been. My section I believe was considered the slowest class and got less attention. One of the guys in the other class talked about all the wonderful things they did in class. When she got to us, we did nothing but sit and stare out the window. I assume she didn't want to repeat herself.

In ninth grade we began to get a little more serious about our education, but for me it was too little too late. My years in junior high had put me behind the eight ball. Once a teacher in ninth grade wanted to know, what was a verb? I was cocky and thought I was smarter than I was. We usually only sat and looked out the window.

"A verb is an action word," I said.

"Give me an example."

"Fast," I said

"No," she said, "could someone else give me an example?

I was outdone. Here I was a freshman in high school and didn't have the parts of speech clearly in my mind.

We had an algebra I class in tenth grade. Again, there were two sections. I believe the class I was in was considered without promise. My feelings were that the teacher would avoid the more difficult problems—further handicapping us.

At that time, I had come to think that the less I worked at doing schoolwork the better off I was. I thought I was scamming the teachers when the teachers were scamming me. I was the biggest loser in that situation.

I recall, in high school civics' class, my teacher said the definition of *laissez faire* was to let alone. She continued to explain that it meant free from government regulation and intervention. Let alone is used here to help explain my childhood relationships to the major forces in my environment.

It seems that my parents and teachers thought the best policy was to leave me alone. There were no other functional organizations or institutions in my so-called community. My parents then left me to basically take care of myself once I was out of diapers. Neither my mother nor father ever provided training, or even basic information to help me survive. My parents never said much unless they felt I wasn't doing the chores right. I was left to roam the hills with the other animals. As I got older, I was truly on my own.

From that point on it was just a matter of being babysat until it was time to graduate. I needed speech therapy because of a speech impediment, but I was intent on going to college. I had thought about going to college for several years. Two other boys were going to college and I wanted to be like them. Besides, I had observed my brothers and other men in the community being unable to get decent jobs and taking what jobs were available. I figured a college education would help me to get a decent job. I made a decent enough score on the ACT test to get accepted to the school I wanted to attend. The rest is history as some would say.

I spent most of my youth plowing a mule from sunup to sunset during the growing season. There was not much time for anything else; but I had to take time to fix fences, cut wood, cut grass, heard cattle, etc. There wasn't time for play or cultivating a personality by socializing with others. The only thing that interrupted my plowing was rain and the changing of the seasons.

I believe my isolation on that dirt farm caused me to have a severe speech impediment and to be under-socialized. My father taking me places and leaving me in the car didn't help my speech or my socialization process. But by then it was a little late to even work on my socialization skills. My relatives talking for me in most situations didn't help my speech or my socialization. This speech impediment resulting from lack of socialization caused me to have many problems in my latter development. Few people in my family spent any time trying to communicate with me. This impediment made it hard for me to express myself or to relate to people in general. I believe that this situation reaped havoc on my self-esteem. It was even difficult for me to freely express myself or relate to females— especially. I was always nervous and anxious—like a coyote, and never felt liked by anyone. I was even doubtful about how my parents, my sisters and brothers, people in the community, or the people I went to school with felt about me. I generally felt people didn't like me.

I knew that Social Security would give me a monthly check because my father retired when I was sixteen. I wasn't sure about the funding but knew I wanted to go to college. So, I went off to college. Again, my historical conditioning had an impact on what I was able to accomplish in school. My isolation and my under-socialized behavior kept me from taking full benefits of that education. At times I would sit in class and be nervously shaking in my boots, out of place, but determined to get that education. My historical conditioning was affecting my ability to take advantage of opportunities long denied. I had been handicapped in many ways but was able to get through college with a "B" average. I had a long way to go in order to overcome my dysfunction. When I graduated college, I had no relatives that I felt comfortable enough to ask for shelter until I could find a job. I had spent my last dime. So, I went the only place I knew to go—back to the country. My parents still lived in the same place and had no transportation. If I had only had a car I would have stayed and sought a job. Though, it was hard for a college level Black person to find a comparable job in nearby towns in 1970. When I went home my mother started to hassle me about plowing in her garden and looking for the cows in the hills. I knew I had to get away. The reason why I went to college was to get away from that type of life.

So, I joined the Navy. I was going to join the Army—anything I could do to get away from the country. The Army rejected me. The Army recruiter said I had a hernia, and to check out the Navy. Later, I heard that I was probably rejected because the Army would have to send me to Officer Candidate School. But in the Navy, unless you met some high educational requirement in addition to a college education, would take you as an enlisted man. To avoid sending me to OCS he simply suggested I try the Navy. This is a part of historical patterns of racism and discrimination that has affected Blacks.

In the military I didn't get along well with a lot of people. Most of my peers didn't seem to care for me. Finally, I became paranoid, started hearing voices, and having streams of consciousness. I never spent time in a psychiatric hospital, except in the military I spent two months on a neuropsychiatric unit. The pressure finally got to me. I feel that my family didn't prepare me for getting along in the world. I should have known from the beginning that the military was not the place for a man with poor socialization skills. The military requires close living and contact with others.

The rest of my family was even more dysfunctional than I was. One sister was fairly intelligent but dropped out early and headed for larger cities. One brother was fairly intelligent but dropped out and headed for the Gulf Coast. Another sister was a good public speaker but dropped out and headed for the big city—she never developed her talent. Another brother was good at drawing but dropped out and headed for the Gulf Coast. One brother was good at just about anything but dropped out and headed for the Gulf Coast. One sister discovered at 62 years of age that she potentially had some skills to be an artist. I couldn't believe the sketches she sent me. The sketches had such attention to detail, strong lines, and dept of perception. I tried to encourage her to pursue art, but she felt it was too little too late. Only two brothers and three sisters graduated high school. This brother who graduated was good at math, but never developed his talent. I was the only one to attend college.

Being kept ignorant and disfranchised for generations is a part of that Post-Traumatic Slave Syndrome: not being able to go to school and get a good education in the twentieth century is a part of what kept my family dysfunctional.

I got several degrees, but still found it difficult to get along with people. After the military I tried to further my education and found the same old problems. I was successful in getting an education, but still had my share of difficulties.

My isolation, historical conditioning, and under-socialized behavior affected my work to a great degree. I finally had to go on disability.

It was only after the devastating post-traumatic experience, and the enforcement of destructive outside cultural conditioning that Africans in America became traumatize. The devastation of being taken from home, enslaved, beaten, and otherwise mistreated, was the cause of this syndrome. Naturally this syndrome would have a long-lasting effect on the personality. My ancestors subsequently passed this trauma on from one generation to another.

It is believed that this Post-Traumatic Slave Syndrome manifested itself in my family. After reviewing some of the symptoms of this Post-Traumatic Slave Syndrome, in the next several chapters I describe exactly how these symptoms were manifested in my family. It is felt that after being exposed to the post-traumas of slavery, individuals will present all or some of the symptoms listed below.

Trans-generational adaptations associated with symptoms of the post-trauma of slavery and on-going oppression:

1). Low self-esteem; 2). Undermining behavior; 3). The setting of unrealistic limits; 4). Poor self-image; 5). Self-hate; 6). Fear, anger, grief, and hopelessness; 7). Loss of dignity and identity; 8). Destroyed bonds and relationships; 9). Feelings of inferiority; 10). Inability to unify as a family; 11). The assumption of failure; 12). Lack of self-confidence; 13). Poor parenting skills; 14). Lack of pride and respect for one's self and others; 15). The tendency of the father to abandon the family; 16). The tendency to see other males and females as the real men and women; 17). Ever-present fear and rage; 18). Lack of feeling secure about self and others; 19). Paranoid against the system; 20). A belief that we have limited choices; 21). Plague by doubts about one's self and others; 22). Limited view of one's potential; 23). Aloofness and instability; 24). Lack of self-worth; 25). Lack of aspirations; 26). Fatalistic attitude; 27). Often self- and other-destructive; 28). Identifying with the oppressor; 29). Belief that Black human characteristics are inferior and that other groups characteristics are superior; 30). Belief that other groups are intellectually superior; 31). Adopting other groups standards of beauty and material success, as well as violence and brutality; 32). Denial that racism exists; 33). Glamorization of lack of education. (All these notions are based on my own empirical observations and experiences: as a social worker for seventeen years.)

<u>Trans-generational adaptations associated with symptoms of the post-trauma of slavery and on-going oppression in our children:</u>

1). Die at a disproportionate rate; 2). Negative habits of all types; 3). Don't know who we are; 4). Internalize negative images in the media; 5). Internalize and adopt negative stereotypes; 6). Discord between young men and women; 7). Expectation of failure; 8). Internalized shame and humiliation; 9). Orchestration of the demise of other Blacks; 10). Hypersensitive to disrespect. (All these notions are based on my own empirical observations and experience; as a social worker for seventeen years.)

7

⚜

My Mother Became Paranoid

After the confusion, chaos, and disorganization of prior conditions in the Black family, it is easy to see how my family became dysfunctional. What else does schizophrenia result from except genetics, confusion, chaos, disorganization, poor environment and mistreatment; and it leads to more of the same. Some would ask, if these conditions are productive of schizophrenia, why aren't all Black families schizophrenic? The situation is that these conditions do not affect all families the same. All families from this period did not exist under the same conditions: some were always free and were able to attend school, and some were given land; some were exposed to less racism, prejudice, bigotry, and discrimination. Psychiatric problems are directly proportional to the amount of pressure a family undergoes over a given period of time. These problems usually depend upon one's genetic inheritance as well as the environmental situation.

A lot of people would wonder why I would speak negatively about my family. After all, one is supposed to honor their father and mother. I don't mean to dishonor either my father or mother. But I personally believe one should honor his father and mother only if his mother and father honored him. Bringing you into the world is not enough. My parents used to say, "I brought you into the world, what more do you want?" In childhood the worse possible offense one could speak against another person was to speak negatively about the person's parents. One could easily get attacked by speaking negatively about someone's parents. I only speak negatively about them because what I say is the truth, and I am all about speaking the truth—no matter who it hurts. In any case, my parents are deceased, and what I say can't hurt them very much. If what I say sounds negative, then so be it. I hold no animosity toward either my mother or father; I merely want to put forth the truth as near as I can figure it out to be. I don't mean to speak negatively about my parents, because some people say, the older they got, the smarter their parents got. This would seem to be partially the case in my situation. My parents simply behaved the way previously acted upon and conditioned by the general conditions of society. I realize that my parents had no specific evil intent for their behavior.

I cannot truly say my mother was paranoid. I can only say that her behavior seemed to reflect that of a paranoiac. Paranoia has been defined as a psychotic disorder characterized by systematic delusions, especially of persecutions or grandeur, in the absence of other personality disorders; extreme, irrational distrust of others; a psychosis characterized by systematic delusions of persecutions or grandeur usually without hallucinations; and a tendency on the part of an individual toward excessive or irrational suspiciousness and distrustfulness of others. She was never to my knowledge diagnosed as paranoid, and no one else in the family said she was paranoid, but I considered her to be a paranoid schizophrenic. This was simply my conclusion. I say she was paranoid because of what I later learned as a psychiatric social worker in a state psychiatric mental health center, while I worked there for a period of seven years—in addition to other mental health experiences. It is also my conclusion that had she not been so isolated her condition would have been more apparent to others and would likely have been a candidate for hospitalization.

Neither my mother nor father engaged in conversations with me very often; conversation was minimal in our family. I personally don't know of any mental illness on my mother's side of the family; if there were any my mother never discussed them. I did hear my mother say that on my father's side of the family a younger brother died from some sort of fits. There was also a brother who would on occasions be admitted to a psychiatric hospital. This is the most I heard about any mental problems in my ancestors.

My mother was born in 1901 on a cold-rainy night in December. It was a small-rural town called Homer, Louisiana; a few miles north of Shreveport, and east of Couchwood, Louisiana; only a few miles away from Homer. My father was born and raised in Couchwood. In those days Blacks rarely gave birth in hospitals but would have a midwife and several ladies in the community to assist with the birth. Blacks had difficulty being admitted to hospitals in those days. In the first place Blacks were usually a great distance from a hospital. When Blacks were admitted most would be given a place by the hot-water heater and the furnace in the basement. In the second place Blacks couldn't afford a hospital. Even if we had a medical card it was still difficult to get treated. It was a long and forced labor. The midwives thought it would be a breached birth, because it was taking so long, but finally my mother's head began to appear. The midwife was soon spanking her. She was a healthy 6 lbs. 9 ounces baby. She was born the fourth child to her mother, out of seven children. She was born into a shotgun, rusty-tin-roof shack. Her father and mother had been able to acquire some land on which this shack stood. Her mother and father owned quite a few acres. Her ancestors had acquired the land soon after slavery. With the help of some home remedies my mother was able to survive her infancy, and on through her childhood.

Of course, the automobile was a number of years from being invented yet. My mother and her parents traveled by horse and buggy, horseback, or wagon. There was nothing but muddy trails throughout the community. My mother learned to take care of the chores on the farm even before she started school, and spent most of her childhood doing chores on the farm.

School was about six miles away from where she lived, and she walked these six miles to and from school every day until she left school after she graduated the eighth grade. Her father and mother didn't promote an interest in school. Consequently, she never felt favorably disposed toward school either, a similar situation to my dad's. In those days, education was seen as extra-curricula activity. All her parents cared about was work on the farm and the sawmill. Slavery wasn't in the far too distant past, and most Blacks didn't expect to benefit from an education. Even if we were lucky enough to get an education, there were few possible jobs for us, because of discrimination. She was more focused on doing the chores at home. Blacks in those days were expected to be happy down on the farm. She continued to live and work on the farm until she met and married my father at the age of twenty-one. Most of the children in school belonged to sharecropper families, and only went to school about six months a year. Even then they got off early during the day to help out on the plantation. My mother said her father was a task master. He made her plow a team of mules during her early years, and would beat her and leave welts all over her body. The boys were needed to work at the local sawmill. The farm work was expendable.

My mother's great-grandparents and grandparents were recently out of slavery and had little education. The school she attended was basically a one-room schoolhouse with one through eighth grades in one room. It was a rusty-tin-roof shack that was heated by a potbellied stove. Of course, air conditioning was a long way from being invented. It leaked through the roof when it rained, and a cold wind could be felt indoors in dead of winter. Cracks were visible through the walls. Black children had to work on the various plantations for most of the year. Plantation work for Blacks took priority over any type of education. She had to walk a number of miles to school each day in order to attend school. Books and supplies, when available, were handed down from the other part of the district, and were usually outdated. The only instructions were in basic math and reading.

The only high school was twenty miles away, and my mother never even entertained the fantasy of being able to attend high school in the city. Her father couldn't afford it, and there was no transportation. There was also little interest on the part of her father and mother. My mother passed on to her children this skeptical attitude toward getting an education.

Once she caught me reading before school and made me get up for several weeks before school and plow before going to school. She had a negative attitude toward reading that can be traced directly to the slave master and his attitude toward slaves getting an education; when he would beat, threaten, maim, or kill slaves if he caught them reading. Her conditioning was so strong that it was still in effect almost a hundred years later. As a result, she didn't promote the education of any of her children. My mother was conditioned to farm work, and it was all she knew.

The fact that Blacks weren't allowed to read in slavery got passed on from one generation to the next, resulting in my mother seeing no place for reading in her household. She had been conditioned to that extent. There were no schools for slaves in slavery. Only the rare slave learned how to read and do math. Only the rare slave master taught his slaves to read. Consequently, my mother and father didn't believe in an education for their children, neither did their parents believe in an education for their children. My parents made little effort to educate their children. Such things got passed on from generation to generation, and can be seen as part of my family's dysfunction.

My mother boasted of not having visited a doctor until she was well into adulthood. Since my mother never got an opportunity to get treatments from medical doctors, it was only natural that she would seek out folk healers. In those days seeing a doctor was something rare, and one had to be near death. Her family mostly survived on home remedies. My mother's mother died when my mother was twelve. Her father later remarried and had four more children. But by this time my mother had met my father and had children of her own.

My mother was happy to graduate the eighth grade. Since there were no high schools nearby, she ended her schooling. Secondary education wasn't encouraged or readily available in rural areas during her youth, and she had to work on the farm to help support the rest of her family. Consequently, my mother didn't seem to think much of an education; work on the farm seemed to be all that was important. She then went to work on the farm. She helped out on the farm until she and my father were married when she was twenty-one years of age. Until my parents got married, she did most of the farm work for her father. She would take care of the farm while her brothers worked at the nearby sawmill. She experienced World War I as a teenager. From what I understand, her father was a taskmaster, and demanded that she run a tight ship on the farm. Her work included handling a team of mules to do the plowing. She vowed to never treat her daughters the way her father treated her. I suppose she had no such conception about the boys, because she made sure they plowed a mule for most of their childhood.

My mother was born before it was legal for women to vote, and probably never voted once in her lifetime. Women gained the right to vote in 1920, shortly before she got married. She was happy in her isolation and her non-participation in civic and community affairs. Life for her was a struggle with getting the basic necessities of life— which she never quite attained. As long as she had rags to wear, food to eat, and a roof over her head she was satisfied.

She was so isolated back in those woods that she began to create her own reality. I could hear my mother when I was growing up talking to imaginary people as well as herself, and we would be at home alone. Sometimes she would get loud, and as a child I didn't know what to think. She would even say as a child that people would accuse her of doing certain things. Also, she said voices would come to her and tell her things. We seldom got visitors, because no one wanted to tackle that trail. Even relatives were reluctant to visit. My mother occupied herself with canning, cultivating the fields, sewing, and overseeing our work on the farm. I don't know when or how my mother began to get paranoid, but she began to get paranoid about a particular neighbor. She would frequently voice paranoid ideations about people in the community.

I remember clearly her paranoia concerning the Taylors. They lived about a mile down the road from us. Their house sat about a hundred feet off the road to the left from our house. The Taylors were always a great mystery to me, and caused my mother much consternation. My mother painted the Taylors as being ominous, crafty, and treacherous. I never figured out whether my mother was excessively paranoid or if the Taylors were doing what she accused them of doing. My mother was not on talking terms with the Taylors. When one of the family fences was down, she accused the Taylors of cutting it; when an animal was injured, she accused them of maiming it; she accused them of turning their animals loose in our fields. If a barn burned, she accused them of setting the fire. Once my horse died and she accused them of poisoning it. A pig came home with a knot on its hip, and the Taylors were accused of hitting it with a stick. A cow came home with a crippled leg, and she accused them of hitting it with a rock.

"Mr. Taylor was the one who did that. He can really throw and hit his mark."

Mr. Taylor had a reputation for being accurate with a rock, at least as far as my mother was concerned.

"Why should he maim a defenseless animal?"

"He has never liked this family. He's trying to get us back for living on this land."

The Taylors were close cousins of my mother. They both lived on land handed down through common ancestors. My mother felt the Taylors were resentful of her living on the land for some reason.

She was forever afraid the Taylors would poison or kill her livestock, and would sneak around at night and set her house on fire. My mother was sure that the Taylors were plotting to put a fix on her family. The Taylors never committed any offense that I could clearly say they were responsible for, but my mother swore they were out to destroy the family and everything around it. Apparently, this feud had its origin many years ago, when my mother and father first moved to where we lived. My mother was afraid to leave home and leave the house unattended for fear they would come around and do some kind of damage. I have no idea why my mother became paranoid against the Taylors. My mother and brother John even went as far as to say they had done something to the land to make it less productive. Whenever I would go by their home, they were quite friendly. My mother must have known something that I wasn't privy to. My mother exhibited paranoia in a number of situations but was mostly fixated on the Taylors.

Most of this behavior is related to the Post-Traumatic Slave Syndrome. My mother was conditioned from the time she was born to be the way she was. The behavior was simply passed on from generation to generation.

Once a neighbor who lived a few miles down the road, he was my mother's uncle, brought her a possum that had been cooked. My mother swore that he had put arsenic in it. I couldn't figure out why he would go to the trouble of putting arsenic in it, then cooking it, and bringing it to her. I felt this was an example of my mother's paranoia.

My mother didn't think that people in general liked her, and that these people were all against her. She felt that certain people would try to voodoo her. A neighbor gave her some fish he had caught, and she voiced paranoia, before reluctantly eating the fish.

She practically had me and everyone else in the family convinced that people were trying to voodoo the family. The truth of the situation was that Black, poor, isolated, and invisible families were under a great deal of pressure to survive. This pressure was enough to cause them to believe in supernatural and superstitious forces such as voodoo. This is what I refer to as "other groups voodoo": it consists mainly of pressure from racism, discrimination, prejudice, and bigotry; in the form of economic, political, social, educational, and psychological pressures.

My mother's background contributed to her paranoid dysfunction, which came out of her historical context. My mother's isolation in part due to historical racism, prejudice, bigotry, and discrimination, all contributed to her dysfunction. A lack of awareness, consciousness, and limited opportunity also contributed to her dysfunction. Her historical background led her to develop a hard ass, slave, sharecroppers, and farming mentality. All she seemed to care about was maintaining that little fifty-acre dirt farm that we lived on. She had no sense of consciousness beyond that farm. Education for her children was not a concern. She would have been satisfied with me plowing in the fields and working around the farm rather than going to school. It didn't matter to her that all we had was a three-mile trail to our house. If necessary, she would try and beat her values into my consciousness. She would beat me just as a slave master would beat a slave, and she thought nothing of working me from sunup to sunset. It also didn't get to hot for me to carry on work in the fields. This is the same way her father had treated her. She made sure she carried on in the tradition of her father, grandfather, and great-grandfather. In this way she promoted a certain psychological tradition as well. In this way she also carried on a historical tradition of the Post-Traumatic Slave Syndrome.

My mother died in 1989. I didn't feel I really knew her. She was eighty-eight-years old when she died. She didn't travel much: she never flew on a plane, rode a train, or a bus. I can count the times she left home on one hand. She never ventured more than 300 miles away from home, and that was at someone's urging. The only place she went with any consistency was to church and to see the voodoo lady. Her ideas were outdated; she was from the old school.

Some would ask the question, how does discrimination, racism, prejudice, and bigotry cause dysfunction and paranoid schizophrenia in a family? But it is the inevitable chaos-confusion-disorganization which can come from discrimination, racism, prejudice, bigotry, genetics, and a poor environment that can lead to the paranoid schizophrenia.

So, my family's schizophrenia didn't directly come from discrimination, racism, prejudice, and bigotry. The schizophrenia came from the confusion, chaos disorganization, genetics, a poor environment, which in some ways accompany discrimination, racism, prejudice, and bigotry.

8

⊂ℨ◆℀⊃

My Father Punked Out

My father was no punk and was a real man—so to speak. When I say he punked out, it has nothing to do with his sexual prowess, but has everything to do with his personal attitude. Punking out is a slang phrase that I have adopted to mean quitting, giving up, or abdicating one's responsibilities. This is the sense in which I speak of my father punking out. There was a time in my community when the word punk implied some type of sexual behavior. Punking out means to quit, especially from fear; to chicken out or back down as from intimidation; scared or frightened to act; back down from a confrontational situation because you are too afraid to act; to display cowardice; and among homosexuals it does still mean in some circles to rape another man. I accuse him of punking out because to me the term best describes my father's situation and attitude. My father punked out on my mom, my sisters and brothers, me, and his responsibilities in general.

My father was born on a hot August night. Like my mother he came with the help of midwives. His birth was quick and sure. He was number eight of sixteen. My father was born in a sharecropper's shack on a plantation. His family spent most of their early years traveling from one sharecropper's situation to another.

My father was raised in a small town called Couchwood, Louisiana. My father only completed the second grade and began to work on the farm. His family needed him to help support the family. It was customary in those days for plantation work to take priority over the children's education. His family made their living going from one sharecropping situation to another. For some reason his family never owned land. They sharecropped on rural farms in the Couchwood area. The school situation was similar to that of my mother's. He never developed much aptitude for school because his family also never promoted an interest in school. He felt he wasn't getting anywhere in school because there was little motivation from his home, and he had to walk a number of miles just to get to school. He helped his family support themselves until he met and married my mother at the age of twenty-two in 1922. His great-grandparents were not long out of slavery. His parents didn't emphasize an education. He only went to the second grade, and subsequently didn't emphasize his children getting an education. He simply passed the idea of not getting an education along to his children.

My father met my mother at a church gathering in the Homer area where my mother was raised. He would drive a team of mules in a wagon from Couchwood to Homer to court her on Sundays— about ten miles away. He talked about how he would sit on one end of the couch while my mother would sit on the other end when he visited her. She was afraid to get close to him. My grandfather warned her to watch out for my father. But the courtship proceeded. It took at least six months before my maternal grandfather would consent to the wedding, but soon gave them his best wishes.

My father was twenty-two and my mother was twenty-one

when they got married. My parents at first worked as sharecroppers on various plantations. Several of the plantations were owned by Black men.

My mother and father were third-generation sharecroppers out of slavery; with all the concomitant historical, social, political, psychological, and educational baggage—innate intelligence not an issue. Consequently, my mother and father never developed a mentality beyond that of a sharecropper, and never saw how an education could benefit any of their children. Some parents capitalized on their deprivation, and wanted better for their children, while others took the attitude that education was unnecessary.

After my mother and father were married, they spent time in a number of sharecropping situations in and around Homer, living in shacks on plantations. Finally, in 1929 with a baby on the way, at the beginning of the Depression, my mother wanted to settle on a piece of family land and build a home—so they did. This land was located in the rural area of Homer. My mother's maternal grandparents had farmed this piece of land. My father consented, so they built a tin-roof shack made of recycled lumber on a fifty-acre parcel of land that was handed down through her mother's side of the family. The land was located three miles off the highway. The highway ran north and south. Our property was three miles due west of the main highway. The main highway was a curvaceous, hill-ridden, two-lane, meandering—black-topped road. It ran north to Homer (5,000) and south to Shreveport (200,000). Monroe was East of Homer (130,000), Alexandria was south (40,000), and New Orleans was south (600,000). Marshall, Texas was to the north (45,000).

My mother and father couldn't afford new lumber. New lumber was hard to come by, so they tore down an old house a few miles away, hauled the lumber by wagon, and built the house. Several men from the community and a jackleg carpenter built the house. This was common in those days. My parents used what they had. Most people in the area existed under similar conditions.

Things were scarce during the Depression, but my parents were use to scarcity. It was even more difficult trying to start a family during the heart of the Depression. My parents at least grew enough food to feed themselves. Things were also scarce during World War II. They got use to doing with only the basics: just food, clothing, and shelter. Things were also scarce during World War I, but at that time my mother was living at home with her father. My mother and father's experience of two world wars and the Great Depression were enough to give them a fugal mentality.

My father farmed from 1922 until 1947. This was the year I was born. He headed for the Gulf Coast soon after I was born. He would also do odd jobs for other people for most of that period. The time came when it got too difficult for him to take care of his family by farming and doing odd jobs. He also got tired of negotiating that trail trying to get to a job in the nearest town. My mother had found her dream and wasn't about to leave it: she had a shotgun shack, something to eat, and clothes to wear. She was happy in her isolation. In addition, I understand my mother was becoming more difficult for my father to live with.

I also heard members of my family say a man was making inappropriate advances to my mother, and my father drew a shotgun on him. The man told my father if he didn't leave, he would kill him.

In addition, my mother had been angry at my father since early in their marriage. My mother's father remarried. My mother's youngest sister came to live with them; she had difficulty getting alone with the stepmother. My mother was the oldest girl, so this sister came to live with her. My father was supposed to have gotten my aunt pregnant. My father denied it, but years later I saw a picture of the child, and he looked exactly like my father. This is just my opinion. If it's true it was the first instance of my father punking out. This created some hard feelings on the part of other family members for my father. My mother and father's relationship, I don't think, has ever been the same.

The next time he punked out was when he let my mother dress me in my sister's hand-me-down dresses until I was three years old.

My mother was burnt out and believed in making do with what she had. She knew nothing about human behavior, or what effect this would have on my personality. There were two girls before me, and my mother simply made do. Clothing was also scarce during World War II and the Depression. My father, being the leader of the family, should have directed her toward the correct behavior.

My father took a job on the Gulf Coast. But it was a good time to take such a job. Jobs were plentiful on the Gulf Coast, and there were few jobs for an unskilled laborer in North Louisiana. You might say my father punked out on his responsibilities and his family. He left his wife and his children to survive on their own. Even though he didn't like his job situation, it is a difficult thing to do—to leave your wife and family under any circumstances. He did come home consistently twice a month and spent his summer vacations fixing up the farm. He still wasn't the stable role model he could have been. It is my estimation that about this time my mother's psychiatric health took a turn for the worst. This is just my estimation. It could have begun to decline prior to this situation.

My dad liked chasing pretty women, drinking expensive whiskey, and was generous with them to a fault. I'm not sure if he indulged in gambling. I don't remember him talking about gambling, and I was never around to see him doing it. Chasing women, drinking, and gambling was about the only excesses a Black man was allowed to engage in. It was limited as to what activities a Black man could engage in those days. Black men were discriminated against and disfranchised in so many ways. Without these releases, given the situation, many Black men would have imploded.

My father drank heavily in order to forget the circumstances in which we lived. One cold winter night he got drunk on his trip from the Gulf Coast to the country, fell in a ditch and dislocated his shoulder, on a moonless night. He had to stay there all night until some community people helped him home. They also helped to pop his shoulder back into place. He was lucky that a wild animal didn't find and attack him. In the earlier part of his life my father drank heavily, but later drank more socially.

I heard him speak of some of his women, and saw him, even in his older age, drink his kidneys into renal failure. He must have realized that our situation wasn't a good one to be in. All the while he was trying to get my mother to move to the Gulf Coast, but she refused to move. She felt that he might get her in the city and leave her, so she decided to remain where she knew the condition was stable. I once overheard a limited conversation about this situation between my mother and father.

"Let's move these children to the coast, Susie—life will be better for them there," demanded my father.

After that I had my doubts about whether my father was serious or just putting on a show.

"I'm not leaving my home and land to go to a place I know nothing about," my mother said, "you're not going to get me in some strange place and leave me."

"I haven't left you in all these years, why do you think I'd leave you now?"

My mother was insecure and paranoid. She was comfortable on the farm, and knew she couldn't take care of herself in the city. She had never done any work except farm work, feared the necessity of having to get a job, and take care of her own needs.

"I don't know if I can trust you. I had better stay here where I know I have a place of my own."

I kept thinking how nice it would be to abandon that isolated farm.

I went to visit my father when I was six years of age on the Gulf Coast. I went back several years later. He placed me in the care of his friend's son. The son was several years older than I. It was apparent by the way my father related to this family that he had something going with them. Later when he came to visit, he brought them sacks of potatoes and vegetables that we had raised on the farm. My mother thought he was taking them to sell, but he was giving them away to this family. The husband would come home and find my father grinning like a Cheshire cat. My assumption was that my father was too valuable for the man to lose. My father was helping him to pay his bills, and my cousins and brothers said some of the children were my father's biological children. Again, my father punked out.

Tonight, it was June 1960. My father had come home on one of his every two weeks visits. But there was something different about tonight. I woke up and saw that he had brought three of his children with him for a visit. I was thirteen and in seventh grade. There was Tim, Carol, and Jimmy: Carol was the oldest, sixteen; Tim was twelve; and Jimmy was nine. Jimmy and Tim were good baseball players, and Jimmy was also a good dancer. It was actually about 10 p.m. when they arrived. We went to bed quite early in those days. They say if you give the devil enough room, he will show his hand. That's what my father was doing that night. I spoke to them, knowing my mother would be upset.

"Hey homeboy, what's going on?" I asked, shaking his hand.

"Not much, man," Tim replied, patting me on the shoulder with the other hand.

"What brings you guys up to the farm?" I asked, as I sat on the bed.

"Just wanted to visit," Tim said, as he took a seat in the chair next to the bed.

I showed them where they could bunk for the night. We all could hear my mother and father arguing back and forth until late in the night. It was probably obvious to my mother that these were his children; they were all the spitting image of him. I couldn't believe the children would follow him three-hundred miles to a place they had never been, but children will follow some adults anywhere. What was there mother thinking? I drowned out most of the conversation, but allowed one bit of conversation to puncture my consciousness.

"Are these your children?" my mother asked, I could hear her through the un-insulated walls.

"These kids belong to a neighbor. I've been telling them I was going to take them to see my farm. They wanted to know what it was like on a farm," my father said.

"Sure."

"All that stuff is just in your imagination."

"It's not just in my imagination. I told you your shit would eventually catch up to you."

"I told you the truth. Now get some sleep. I'm tired from my trip."

At that point I cut them off, but my mother ranted and raved all night. One thing was true: my father was a lover and not a fighter. He was not going to let my mother goad him into a fight, so he cut it off. My mother kept crying and arguing throughout the night. She did stop arguing at breakfast long enough to get some food on the table for all of us, but you could see in her attitude that she was still upset. She pouted and puffed all morning; until my father decided he wanted to go into the town of Homer.

He came into the room and said, "Get ready, let's go to Homer." We all said, "OK."

The kids took it in stride. I can't really tell what the children were thinking. But they certainly knew what my mother was thinking, but never said a word to me about my mother. To this day we never discussed the situation.

We walked to the end of the dirt road and caught a ride with a neighbor who just happened to be going to Homer. We walked the streets until my father finished his shopping. Then we left. My father acted as if he didn't care; as if he expected my mother to react this way. To this day I don't know what prompted my father to bring them home. He seemed to consider himself "king-on-the-throne." From what my brothers said this relationship had gone on for twenty years or more. We came back home and my mother was still pouting. She again reluctantly fixed lunch. That night they argued some more. This time I covered my head with a pillow so as not to hear the screaming and crying. My dad was steadfast about not physically fighting with my mother.

I don't think they resolved anything that night, but on Sunday evening the man who dropped them off was there to pick them up. My father should have known the effect this would have on my mother. He had been involved so long that he had forgotten himself.

My mother forgot her manners and didn't say good-bye to the children. She went out on the back porch until they left. I never discussed the implications of my mother's rage with any of them. We all just accepted the whole thing as the price of doing dirty business. I never saw any of these kids again until I was out of college, and never again visited my father in Bluefield, Texas. I don't believe that my mother and father had the same relationship ever again. Once again, my father had completely punked out. My mother wasn't just paranoid; there was something strange about him bringing these three children home with him who resembled him a great deal. I don't know if he thought my mother was that ignorant or just oblivious as to what was going on. But he must have thought he could get away with it without too much fanfare.

I felt closer to my father than anyone else in the family, but I really wasn't close to him either. My father was getting older as I grew up; he was forty-five years old when I was born. We never talked much. He never encouraged me to get an education or socially. He didn't take me places with him. When he did take me places, he would leave me in the car while he went inside. He never came to school to see how I was doing. All he ever had to say was to remind me of my duties around the farm. I believe his expectations were that we would all eventually drift away from the educational system and find some type of job.

My father didn't care much about educating his children. But this family my father was involved with had several older boys who were attending college. My cousins and my brothers insisted that my father was helping to send them to school. In this way he punked out on his family responsibilities. My brothers and cousins say he chose the family on the coast over his family in East Texas. The family on the Gulf Coast was more important to him than his family in North Louisiana. He did care enough to buy me a secondhand car while I was in college.

My father also punked out when he failed to teach his children mainstream values: he never tried to teach any of his children about ways of the world, or the boys about how to be a man or function in society, he never took us places or tried to give us a definite set of values, and he never took us places like he was serious about our development—not even fishing or to sporting events. In this way he also punked out. He didn't seem to think one way or another about such things. My father's lack of involvement promoted the Post-Traumatic Slave Syndrome to yet another generation. The son is likely to be much like the father.

My father finally retired in 1962. He received a bonus upon retirement. My cousin says he went to his girlfriend's house and challenged her children to scramble for hundred-dollar bills as he threw them on the ground. This was clearly a punk out, as many needs as we had on the farm, he could afford to do this. I asked him about it several years later. He said he didn't have to give women money; that they gave him money. He said at one time he was known as the master plumber, and that if you were good women would give you money. I knew he was trying to play me off and that he probably did it.

He never tried hard to make things better for us on the farm. We got a road constructed when I was in first grade and electricity soon after that. We got a butane stove and heaters when I was a freshman in high school. We were finally able to get a telephone while I was in college, and later plumbing after I left home for good. He never tried to build a better house or better our surroundings. When I was home my father never even bought us toilet paper. He of course punked out again.

He didn't try hard enough to get my mother to move to the

city. It was during the Great Migration, and people were moving to larger cities. My mother would probably have moved had he given her enough incentive. Everyone was doing it, but again, my father punked out.

My father retired in 1962 and came home supposedly for good, but he couldn't stay at home. He spent his time between the Gulf Coast and North, Louisiana. Sometimes he would spend short periods on the Gulf Coast, and at other times he would spend longer periods. My mother's paranoia had become impossible to adjust to. Again, he punked out on my mother. By this time, my mother was virtually on the farm alone, everyone else had left, and he would leave her to spend time on the Gulf Coast.

My father's misbehavior and punking out, I feel, had its origins from the fact that slaves were used as breeders in slavery, and was unable to form a family, but went from plantation to plantation. My father and mother were some of those who exhibited the Post-Traumatic Slave Syndrome. This conditioning got passed on from one generation to another. The slave master was a sort of pimp; he pimped both the Black male and female. Black men attempted to imitate the slave master by pimping the Black female. Black men and women used each other for sex and then moved on. Instead of getting attached men had sex and moved on; they couldn't form long-lasting relationships. There was no real intimacy involved. Black men became conditioned to this process, and since that time has rejected long-term relationships,

My father believed in having other relationships than the primary family relationship. Lots of men have relationships with more than one woman even if they are married. It is believed that this particular behavior so frequent in Black men is in many cases related to the Post-Traumatic Slave Syndrome, where men were not allowed to get married but only to breed their women. My father's behavior was simply passed on from one generation to another, resulting in his past behavior (Billingsley, 1968, *Black Families in White America*).

My father's not being willing to provide for his children to get an education and his philandering result from his ancestor's unstable role in slavery. Slavery limited my parents and influenced their willingness to settle for poverty and lack in a shack at the end of a three-mile trail.

Slavery denied Black men the role of family responsibility. Male slaves were sent from plantation to plantation, breeding various females. The Black male was used as a stud. The slave master made decisions for the Black family. This scenario has simply been passed on from generation to generation.

Male slaves were not allowed to take responsibility in the family and were demeaned and degraded in front of the family. This conditioning from generation to generation resulted in my father's philandering and abandoning his children—in effect punking out.

My father seemed quite normal as far as appearances go. To my knowledge he never had any psychiatric problems. He simply had a habit of drinking and chasing women. I did often wonder why he never tried to build a better house for us to live or give us one with all the modern conveniences. We called my father Larry; he had no nickname that we called him. Some of my brothers did appropriately call him John. Nicknames weren't very common in our family. He finally died in 1988 from some kind of complications with his kidneys. I remember shedding a few tears when he died, but my father was never much of a father in my life. I figured it was because of his heavy drinking in his early days; he was eighty-eight years old when he died. My father probably rode a bus, but never flew on a plane or rode a train, and never went more than 300 miles from home during his lifetime. I felt like I never really knew him, but next to my brother John, he was the closest thing to a role model I had. When my father died my mother called me in Chicago and said, "Larry's gone." I never really knew him, so I had little feeling for a real person when he died. I had a few tears for him, but never felt that close to him.

9

CB♦CS

Schizophrenic Dysfunction and Function in My Family

Since my mother was what I call a paranoid schizophrenic, it is no wonder that most of her children had some degree of pathology. It is my estimation that she passed it on genetically, through interacting with her children on a daily basis, or passed on hormones through the placenta. I realize that it takes two people with the recessive trait for schizophrenia to be manifested. It also takes an environment with a certain degree of pathology. My father never had any mental health issues I am aware of, except for chasing women and drinking; he also had a problem with providing the necessary education for his children. Apparently, he possessed a recessive trait for schizophrenia.

We had several cases of mental illness in my immediate family. Living in such an isolated environment may have contributed to some of the psychiatric problems.

My mother was under a great deal of pressure being isolated in her initial situation with a tyrannical father. She could have simply passed her behavior along to her children through persistent contact with them.

The family, the school, the church, and the community are the important elements in a person's development. The family is the most important between the family, school, church and community. The family promotes the development and well being of the child. If the family, church, school, and community are dysfunctional; chances are it's going to produce a dysfunctional individual. Having a poor family, community, and educational background caused my parents to be dysfunctional. And this dysfunction simply got passed on from one generation to another.

Several members of my family developed psychiatric disorders. Though, I couldn't put a label on it at the time, I would later refer to these disorders as schizophrenia. It was frustrating at such a young age to see family members in this condition. Sometimes in my private moments I would cry. I knew there was a stigma attached to mental illness even at this young age. There was no attempt to shield me from any of this, nor did anyone try to explain the nature of the problem. My parents knew as little as I did about the problem. I was able to see and hear the symptoms; as well as policemen taking family members out in handcuffs when they became too difficult to manage. One day Jack had to be restrained by a policeman because he didn't want to go with him. Jack had begun acting strange, and my father had gone to town to summon the police. I went into my room and cried. I had seen my family members wrestle and hassle with my brother Lewis and sister Betty as well. My two brothers and one sister who had this problem eventually found their way home to convalesce during their illness. I felt ashamed of them. I would get upset whenever anyone asked how they were doing, or their names were mentioned. In such a small community everyone knew every detail about everybody. I felt that it would've been better for them to go some place else instead of invading my territory with their illness. I often wondered what was wrong with my family. I wondered if this was genetic and would this happen to me eventually. What did neighbors, relatives, friends say or think of the family, or me individually.

First, my third oldest sister, Betty, became ill in July 1951. I have only two recollections of Betty prior to her illness. The first was seeing her come home from school in a plaid-red skirt, black blouse, and penny loafers one day. My mother was talking to her about school. This was before there was a graded road to our house. The other was when she insisted that I not move or make a sound while sleeping and lying in bed next to her. She left home after graduation from high school and got married. The next thing I remembered was that she was living in a distant city and had a child. I remember her coming home on several occasions from the city. Later, she couldn't function as a wife and mother. She came to live with the family for a while. Her three-year-old daughter alternated between living with the family and her father. The three-year-old girl was very talkative, and my brother John would leave her at home because wherever she went, she'd start talking about her mother. My mother seemed to enjoy using her to initiate conversation, but this made John very uneasy. One day at church Betty's little girl participated in such a conversation.

"Is that Betty's little girl?" inquired a church member.

"Yes, it is," replied my mother.

"Where is her mother?" asked the church member, as if she didn't already know.

"My mother is in the hospital," the little girl replied. "Mother is very sick."

"What's wrong with your mother?" asked the church member.

At that point my mother went into her act and told the whole story.

I remember Betty talking to herself, looking sad, and acting otherwise bizarre. I remember seeing her putting a huge piece of cold butter on a slice of white bread and eating it. She just couldn't gather the energy to carry out her day-to-day activities. She'd lie around and sleep most of the time. She was easily agitated. For a long time, out of ignorance, I blamed my brother-in-law for my sister's problems. I blamed him because of conversations I'd heard between my brothers. A rumor was going around in the family that this brother-in-law had said the whole family was crazy. Much unnecessary anger and hostility were indirectly projected toward him. One night, Betty and her husband came to visit. The house caught fire, and my mother accused the brother-in-law of starting the fire. She never accused him to his face, but certainly indicated that she thought he did it. The fire had started in the room where they were sleeping. My brothers said it looked as if someone had tied rags together and set them on fire. I felt that all our lives would have been better off had the house burned to the ground. In this case "burning down the barn to get rid of rats" could have been justified, since the barn was part of the problem. Rats ran through the house openly.

Once my brother-in-law bought my mother some expensive bath towels for Christmas, and somehow my mother got paranoid that he had placed a "fix" on the towels in order to affect her in a negative way. She took the towels to the voodoo lady to undo the "fix," and she never got the towels back. It was a scam on the part of the voodoo lady.

Even I was angry at my brother-in-law for destroying Betty's life. Naturally, when these things occur, people try to find a scapegoat in which to blame the problem. In actuality, I believed he loved her very much. My mother said a neighbor had put a "fix" on Betty because she was aloof, distant, and thought she was better than the neighbor. It amazed me that my family attempted to blame the schizophrenia in the family on voodoo. My mother's answer to schizophrenia was to get treatments from the voodoo lady. She was always vigilant to the idea that someone was trying to voodoo her family.

Lewis developed a mental condition in October 1952. He had been married for several years and had a child. He had spent time on the Gulf Coast and in other cities, but eventually came back home. He always seemed to have an adjustment problem. Lewis stayed unemployed most of the time. He was never able to get a decent job and was sure the world and everybody in it was against him. This was part of the general paranoid pattern in the family. The only obvious symptoms I observed in Lewis were that he became upset with me once, and thought that my youngest sister and I were plotting against him. He became belligerent.

"Don't come in my room," he said. "I know you and Debra are scheming against me."

"W-what do you mean?" I asked.

"You know what you're doing—get out."

"Mama said, get your clothes off the floor."

"I don't care what Mama said, if you don't get out of here, I'll beat your butt," he said vigilantly.

"Forget it, man."

The family worried about Lewis because he'd leave and stay gone for several weeks without any notice of his whereabouts. He had a habit of sleeping in an old car sitting about fifty feet from the house, rather than coming in the house and going to bed. When he did come in the house to bed, he'd sleep with his clothes and shoes on.

"How come you sleep in that old car rather than come in the house and go to bed?" I asked.

"Don't worry about it. Do I get into your business? I do as I please."

Not knowing his state of mind, I continued, "You shouldn't sleep in your shoes and clothes at night. How come you do that?"

"Man, I told you not to worry about me."

Before I knew it, Lewis was choking me. When he let me go, I ran into the yard and across the field. I never bothered him again. He'd also spend a great deal of his time sleeping. Lewis tried but he couldn't serve as a role model, because he was too wrapped up in his own problems. He couldn't see his way clear from day to day. He had no energy to invest in another person. He was too concerned about what the world owed him. He cast himself in the role of a loser and pitiful victim, who needed sympathy and support, because he had experienced such difficulties in his life. He never forgave his mother for making him spend his youth on the farm. I heard him call our mother a slave driver. Basically, in my presence, all he ever talked about was what she did to him; he couldn't seem to forget or get over the idea that he'd been victimized.

"That slave driver ruined us all," he would say.

"What do you mean?"

"I could've been somebody if I had been allowed to go to school rather than having to catch that mule."

"Couldn't you do something else?"

"I didn't know what else to do. There was nowhere for me to go, I had to do whatever she said. I'll never forgive her for that."

He spent a long time in convalescence. He stayed with the family for several years. He spent his time fishing, hunting, and roaming the hills. I never quite understood Lewis, mainly because he mostly kept his thoughts to himself. This was another common trait of the family. None of them ever had much to say, at least when I was around.

Once I was taking Lewis to Shreveport. We got about halfway, and he looked over his shoulder and said in a loud voice, "I'm coming." I didn't know what to think but knew basically what was going on.

Again, my mom encouraged them all to seek treatments from the voodoo lady. She would even take them to see the voodoo lady. She was so sure someone had placed a "fix" on her family, and that the voodoo lady could treat the problem.

Jack developed a problem after being released from the military in September 1953. I was more certain that Jack had a schizophrenic condition. Jack's condition was clearer, and I was older and could clearly remember his symptoms. They all were able to go on with their lives at a later point except Jack. My fear was that Jack experienced a more difficult trauma than the rest of the family. Psychologically he must have been more delicate. He never seemed to become functional again after his initial break. Jack would take flight and get lost in the woods.

Jack was sure that people were burning buildings down and coming for him. He often spoke of the FBI being after him. One day he explained his suspicions to me.

"They're coming to get me."

"What did you say?"

"The FBI is burning down all the buildings going from house to house to find me."

I didn't say anything else because of not wanting to push the conversation.

"I have to go," Jack said. "They'll be here soon." He was nervously pacing and agitated.

"Where're you going?"

"I have to get ahead of them."

My mother tried to stop him, but he pushed her away and ran through the yard, across the field, and into the cow pasture, headed toward the forest. We didn't see him for several weeks. When he came home, he had lost at least one-hundred pounds. He was obese to begin with but returned to normal size. He would sometimes roam the woods for several days, at times getting lost. Once a neighbor found him on the highway; he had been wondering for several weeks. Jack went into the state hospital periodically, because he decided that his medication was no longer necessary. Jack would put out much effort but couldn't seem to get his act together. I could see the remoteness and pain in Jacks eyes, a certain blank stare, long before he left home for the military. At first Sam and John made several attempts to take Jack into their homes and help him get a job; Jack didn't respond well. The whole family made frequent visits to see him in the hospital, but we all figured it was too little too late. He had become paranoid against his medication. My mother insisted that someone had put a "fix" on him and that the voodoo lady could help him.

It is believed that the pathological atmosphere in my family, caused by current and historical factors, was responsible for the dysfunction in my family. Two of my brothers needed psychiatric hospitalization on many occasions. Several other family members had problems that were borderline, but were able to function in a marginal way, though they may not have been disturbed enough for the psychiatric hospital.

My brother, John, was a good person, but had problems of his own. He was at times paranoid and preoccupied with voodoo, and with other people trying to put a "fix" on him. He spent a lot of time evading those who would try to put a spell on him. He spent a lot of time visiting the voodoo lady and wasting a lot of time engaging in rituals concerning voodoo. For example, some woman down the road worked in a cleaner in Shreveport, and he gave her some clothes to clean for him. But later he felt she had put some type of "fix" on his clothes. He planted a field with some corn and potatoes a few miles down the road. When the fields proved to be practically barren, he felt that the land had been fixed by a neighbor to assure the fields would be unproductive. The voodoo lady encouraged him to think in this direction. He would burn candles to ward off evil spirits, and often travel many miles to see the voodoo lady. He would take baths in saltpeter and sprinkle black pepper and salt in his shoes and other of his belongings. He engaged in many senseless rituals.

John once told me that my mother was trying to put something deleterious in my food. He encouraged me not to eat at home but to buy what I needed from the store. He gave me a wad of money big enough to choke a horse for this purpose. I tried fixing my food at a neighbor's house, but I think the neighbor told my father what I was doing. I eventually discontinued the practice. My folks probably thought something was wrong with me, but in reality, I was simply internalizing the general paranoia in our family. John could have spent some time in a psychiatric hospital, but I was for the most part out of touch with him.

John's comfort zone led him to seek residence in the most decrepit ghetto conditions. He was known to change residences and jobs often. The last time I visited him he was living in an old shack a few feet from a railroad track, in the middle of the city, in kind of an isolated spot. I lost contact with him and hadn't seen him since. He was known to drink heavily, as well as use other drugs.

He picked up the use of rituals from the voodoo ladies that my mother encouraged him to visit; to undo the spells that others had placed on him. John went from one voodoo lady to the other; being assured if one didn't help him the other would. My mother in her paranoid state tried to blame all the problems in the family on voodoo. I'm sure she failed to mention all the things she was paranoid about. She probably kept many of her thoughts to herself; being exceptionally good at non-communication.

My knowledge of my mother's suspicious behavior is somewhat limited, since we never went anywhere together, and I was never around when she was in the company of other people. My understanding of her paranoia comes from what I heard her say in private conversations. She would frequently voice suspicion about people trying to place hexes on her and the rest of the family. Sometimes when other people gave her food, she was afraid to eat it.

My mother was paranoid enough to be one of those who would say, "Humpty Dumpty didn't fall, he was pushed."

Another brother, Sam, had only one problem aside from being basically insane—for lack of a better term. He didn't have any schizophrenic symptoms that I was aware of, but he could be violent and had a volatile temper. Sam could be violent and aggressive: he would cut or shoot someone at the drop of a hat. I heard he often beat his wife, and I never knew for sure, but seemed to remember hearing my father and mother say that Sam had killed a man either with a knife or a gun. The person he had killed was non-black, and a Black man had to be crazy to kill a person who was non-black. My mother said, "He would've gone to prison if his boss hadn't gotten him off." They talked about how he was always cutting or shooting at his wife and other people. She had the scars to prove it. Sam had a reputation of being a lady's man, but I never saw him live up to that reputation. My mother, who was prejudice against dark-skin women, would say that Sam always developed a relationship with the blackest and ugliest woman he could find. My mother equated black with ugly. Sam had a reputation for being a lover of "tramps" and "sluts." Again, my mother used these words to describe all women with true African characteristics.

I witnessed Sam trying to cut my sister Martha's throat early one Christmas morning. At the time I was only about four-years old, and was not sure what led up to the incident, but my mother and father said that Sam had been drinking and smoking funny cigarettes. Both Sam and Martha had come home for Christmas. At the time there was nothing but a trail to our house.

"You think you're better than the rest of us, don't you?" Sam said to Martha. He was looking wild and crazy.

"That's crazy, man," Martha replied.

"I see you holding your head high and speaking proper."

"I try to be myself."

Martha knew Sam had a volatile temper, so she backed away.

He lunged forward, yelling, with the knife raised, "High yellow bitch."

All I saw was the knife go up in the air and come down at Martha's throat. Martha was lucky because my mother threw her arm around her neck. My mother weighed at least 350 lbs, and her arms were fat and wide. Her arm was able to shield and catch the blade, protecting her from the knife. Sam didn't cut Martha's neck, but he made a huge gash in my mother's arm. Blood gushed from my mother's arm and ran all over the floor. I was instantly reminded of how blood gushed when my father would stick a knife in a hog's heart at hog-killing time to draw the blood out of its body. My mother didn't get it stitched until later the next day. The cut had to have twenty stitches. She was lucky it didn't set up gangrene. She lied and said she accidentally cut herself while peeling an apple with a sharp knife. After that incident I turned passive and tried to avoid violence; it placed a permanent trauma on my memory and consciousness. Prior to that incident I would fight at the drop of a hat. After that incident, I would cry if someone acted as if they wanted to fight.

Again, Martha was lucky. If Sam had cut her in the jugular vain in her neck, it would probably have been the end of her life. Since there was nothing but a trail to our house, and one would have had to hitch up a wagon, take her over the rugged trail to the main highway, then try to get her to a hospital in Shreveport. If they had been lucky enough to get her to a hospital, she would probably have had difficulty being admitted. Blacks in those days had difficulty getting admitted to hospitals. She would likely have been dead for a long time before she got to the hospital. Sam could have spent time in a psychiatric hospital. I wasn't in touch with Sam enough to know what was happening with him.

Sam had a lackadaisical attitude with respect to his family's surroundings. He seemed to have been satisfied with maintaining minimal standards for his family. He never purchased a decent house for his family or tried to maintain the one he had. Sam was too busy drinking, gambling, and philandering; anything but being a good family man and taking care of his family responsibilities. He did buy a new car and truck on a regular basis. Sam had a reputation as a ladies' man but I never saw him live up to that reputation. The only thing I did see was some pictures he took with various women in Mexico. He was in a hotel room and had his arms tight around one in particular. He always carried a sharp pocket knife and a pistol. He was also known to chronically drink and gamble. He had a volatile temper.

Four of the girls to my knowledge were relatively free from psychiatric pathology. I left after high school and spent very little time around them, or in communication with them. Even some of them could have spent time in a psychiatric hospital.

As a whole, my brothers and sisters didn't get along very well. If one went to live with the other, both of them soon became disgruntled. Though, I don't think many such invitations were extended. When I graduated from college, I had no place to go, but were reluctant to ask if I could live with any of them until I could get on my feet—so to speak. So, I volunteered for the Navy. If I had gone back to live with my parents, I would have been stuck way out in the country without any means of transportation. I was the only one in my immediate family to attempt college. When I did attempt, of my nine brothers and sisters, only one sister offered me any assistance: she sent me twenty-five dollars near the end of my senior year. They didn't even write to me or keep in contact in any way; they didn't even send me a batch of homemade cookies, of which the ingredients can be found in any modern kitchen. I didn't ask them for any help which might explain part of this situation. If this situation existed between sisters and brothers, you would expect other relatives would be distant also. When I was growing up, I wondered why relatives rarely ever came around. Until I was six there was nothing but a three-mile trail to our house, and only a few would try and negotiate that trail. I could see why we had few visitors. After the road was constructed, it is difficult to say why few people came to visit, except that we didn't have any of the modern conveniences. It seems that neither my mother nor father had a good relationship with their families. Even now, I maintain little contact with relatives. It was apparent that relationships had broken down in my family, and that this breakdown had a long history. I have concluded that this history is related to the Post-Traumatic Slave Syndrome.

The only grandparent I knew was my paternal grandmother. She was cold and unaffectionate. If she wanted to know something about me, she would ask my father. My maternal grandmother died before I was born. My maternal grandfather was alive when I was a toddler, but we had nothing but a three-mile trail leading off the main road to our house. That could have had something to do with why he never visited. When I visited my paternal grandmother, I usually stayed outside. My grandmother was in her nineties and kept her house dark and dingy. I never saw her before I was old enough to drive; at that age I would drive my father to see her. She died while I was away at college. No one bothered to inform me about her death, so I could attend the funeral.

I don't feel it is important for me to go back further than my grandparents to get an understanding of my family's Pos-Traumatic Slave Syndrome. I really can't go back much further than that anyway. I figure if my parents and grandparents were in the condition they were in, there's no sense in going back any further in the family.

Black Americans have stood the test of time more so than any other group in the history of our times. If Herbert Spencer's idea is right that the fittest of a species will tend to survive, it would seem that only the extremely fit Black Americans would have been able to survive all the hostility and abuse. It would also seem that a race of superhuman beings should have been created among Blacks in America. It might be that the strong rebelled and were killed off, therefore only allowing the weak to survive. Maybe Spencer's theory doesn't apply to human beings, or maybe the system hasn't allowed this theory to operate without restraints.

In the face of such overwhelming odds, it is now necessary that we develop unity, cooperation, love, and trust among each other, if we are going to improve our situation, and begin to compete successfully in a capitalistic society. As a society we have many problems that need to be eliminated. This would extirpate many individual problems in the Black family, community, society, and the world. Many Blacks deny the effects of racism, and some simply aren't aware of its conditioned negative effects.

It's probably important to realize that I will never quite get over the dysfunction in my family—neither will my sisters and brothers. We will probably carry certain aspects of this dysfunction with us to our graves. It is also felt that this dysfunction in my family and others is partially caused by pre-slavery, Middle Passage, post-slavery, and modern-day conditions.

10

―――――――――― ⌘◆⌘ ――――――――――

What Must We Do to Rid Ourselves of the Post-Traumatic Slave Syndrome?

There are many things Blacks can do to rid themselves of the Post-Traumatic Slave Syndrome. Below are listed just a few.

1. **Develop love, loyalty, unity and learn to consolidate resources.** All Blacks, wherever we exist in the world, should focus on, work toward, promote, and develop: A) love, B) loyalty, C) unity, and D) consolidation of resources. We should include these objectives in everything we do. **Love.** Many Black social scientists have put forth the idea that historically Blacks have found it difficult to love one another. We have been conditioned away from loving each other and toward hating each other. Our conditioning leads us to believe the qualities of other groups are more esthetic. Self-hate leads us to destroy one another on a daily basis.

Negativity in society causes us to refocus these problems inward on ourselves. We have been conditioned to believe that our qualities, characteristics, and minds are inferior. It's important we learn to love ourselves, so we can have strong individuals, families, and societies—if we can't love ourselves, we won't love anyone else. **Loyalty**. Without love there can be no loyalty. If individuals don't have loyalty for each other they won't work together to build strong families, communities, or societies: individuals won't work together to build strong families, families won't work together to build strong communities, and communities won't work together to build strong societies. Frequently we're loyal to everything and everyone except our own people. We must make loyalty to each other a habit. **Unity**. Without love and loyalty there can be no unity. To build better Black communities and families we must have unity. Individuals, families, nor societies can accomplish much without unity. With unity we can accomplish what it's impossible to accomplish alone. We must develop a common ideology from which we all can work and not function as separate entities. There is strength in unity. **Consolidation of Resources**. Without love, loyalty, and unity, we'll never consolidate our resources. We must learn to consolidate our resources if we are to improve the conditions in the Black family. This means putting our collective resources together. This will require the participation of those with the necessary resources. To build anything requires resources. Many blacks have been conditioned away from working together as a unit, and find it difficult to combine collective resources. One reason we don't combine resources is because of a lack of unity. Without consolidating our resources there can be no accumulation of excess capital. **Take One Brick to the Monument**. If you can't carry a load of bricks, at least take one brick to the monument, for the purpose of building our way out of our worldwide predicament. It's a war for survival, and every person need not do something great, but must function at his or her own level. No one will be asked to do more than he or she is capable. All that is asked of every person is to prepare and be ready to make a contribution. **Forget Negativity**. We should for once forget our negativity, personal petty issues, self-hate, and work on positive-grand collective issues. We learned in slavery to have an "individual self-reference" rather than a "social self-reference" (Kardiner & Ovesey 1962 in *The Mark of Oppression*). We've focused for too long on individual self-aggrandizement. It's time to change all that. We should think about how we can improve the Black family. We will never progress until we can learn to work together.

2. **Develop pride in ourselves and our families**. Without pride in each other and our families it is difficult to accomplish any given objective. We have lost our group-identity and self-awareness. We have noting but hate for one another because we have been conditioned to dislike our basic characteristics. It is time to have respect for our characteristics as a group. We like nothing Black and feel that all things Black are inferior.

3. **Come to grips with the fact that we've been hoodwinked, brainwashed, bamboozled, and ran amuck**. Admit the truth regarding the fact that African Americans have been programmed. Many African Americans are not willing to undergo this requirement necessary in eliminating this syndrome, that is, to admit that we have been programmed by other groups to respond in a negative manner. Others may not have known the consequences of this programming process; they may not have given it that much thought or didn't care one way or the other. However, enlightened groups had to know that the outcome would not be favorable for African Americans. It is felt by the author that

other groups knew their treatment would have a devastating effect upon the African American family; although, they probably didn't know how long the family would survive, and the exact ultimate consequences. Regardless, African Americans seem to feel that it would be an insult to admit that other groups could deceive them so successfully. This is precisely what happened: the greatest deception in history was executed. We must admit that this happened and move toward ensuring that it doesn't continue. It is important to understand why and how this happened and attempt to recondition our minds and those of our children. Some African Americans and other groups will quickly defend other groups and emphasize the negative things that we are doing to ourselves. The "Unseen Hand" that has been referred to throughout history tends to reach in and keep the process going. Most people don't see this "Unseen hand," and therefore we say that there are very little negative effects coming from outside the group (Ralph Epperson, 1985, *The Unseen Hand*). However, it is obvious to anyone who is not in extreme denial that there has been and continues to be insidious racism, prejudice, and discrimination. It is crucial to admit as individuals and as a group that this programming has taken place, and that this conditioning, racism, prejudice, and discrimination are real, not just a figment of a few people's imagination.

4. **Get control of our schools, and teach our own educational, social, economic and political theories.** Our schools are being run by outside groups, sometimes these groups do not care about the education of our children. It is up to us to give our children a sufficient education to succeed in society. Other groups' theories sometimes have less application to our children. We must develop our own theories that apply to our children and use them to develop our children according to our educational needs.

Develop our own psychological, political, social, and economic theories. We have found that other's theories can be politically, socially, and educationally bankrupt. We need theories that fit the needs of our children in a twenty-first century world.

5. **Take a larger role and responsibility in training and educating your children.** Each parent must take responsibility for seeing that children are prepared for school. Such things as seeing to it that children get to bed on time, do homework, turn off the TV while doing homework, get to school on time, have a disciplined attitude while at school, visit the school and see how children are doing, and help them to apply themselves to the subject at hand.

6. **Be sure your children know history.** Many African Americans do not realize the nature of the processes that took place, because we haven't studied history in sufficient depth. If we are cut off from our true history, we can never fully understand what effect this history has had on us. Before we can progress, we must reconnect with our history. It is almost impossible to understand other groups, or African Americans simply by relying on one's personal experiences, or only the media for clarification. It is a proven fact that information from various media sources is usually slanted for the benefit of those in control of the system: those with money, influence, and power. We must read African and other groups' history and read it for the truth; one book or one author will not suffice. "History is a clock that tells a people their historical time of day. It is a compass that people use to locate themselves on the map of human geography. A people's history tells them where they have been and what they have been, where they are and what they are. More importantly, a proper understanding of history tells a people what they must be and where they must go" (Clarke, 1991, p. 342, *Notes for an African World Revolution: Africans at the*

Crossroads). We must understand our history in order to see our place in the world. History, it must be understood, is only the beginning and not the ending; it is the place where individuals must start if trying to find themselves. If you don't understand the past, you have no future.

7. **We must develop cooperation and a strong commitment to our families; if we are to develop well-ordered communities and societies.** We need to return to our values of self-love, self-appreciation for family, and a concept of unity (Clarke, 1991, *Notes for an African World Revolutions: Africans at the Crossroads*). We must learn to love ourselves. Without being able to love ourselves, we can love no one else. Once love of self is achieved this love can be generated to family and community. At the present time there is a deficiency in the area of self love. We have lost touch with ourselves, and don't know who or what we have become. A strong sense of who we are as a people would enhance our self-esteem; a strong sense of self would help to cultivate who we are as a family and as a collective. Out of a sense of self, family, and community evolves a concept of unity as a people. The programming process has impeded our ability to engage in building unity. The solution to improving our situation lies in being able to reprogram ourselves.

8. **Join organizations that work to promote the progress of Black people.** A community develops because of its organizations and institutions. It takes the effort of everyone in the community for the maximum development of that community. If every man is waiting on the next man nothing will get done. We are greater as a family and collective if we do things collectively.

9. **Patronize Black businesses.** On last check Black Americans spent 700 billion dollars a year outside the Black community on a yearly basis. We spend very little in the Black community. A dollar turns over few times before it

leaves the Black community. In other communities a dollar turns over many times before it leaves the community. We can't build our communities unless we spend money in our communities. When we spend money with other groups, they use it to build their communities, and leave our communities to die.

10. **Create institutions to help develop the community and maintain control of them.** We have never had control of our own institutions. With the church being one possible exception of having limited control. Our schools are not run by African Americans, which is one of the basic institutions in any community. The economics and politics are certainly controlled from outside the community. Without this control, we cannot determine our own destiny. We must have control of values, norms, mores, and folkways, and ideas being allowed to penetrate the consciousness of our community. We must have control of our own institutions if we are going to control and be responsible for the behavior of individuals within the community. Institutions are the building blocks of a community. Control of these institutions is necessary if transmission of culture is expected to take place. Without control over basic institutions within a community, children simply lose the way, and become victims of anyone who desires to bring about influence. Developing our own institutions helps us to have control of our own agenda. Institutions provide continuity for a people. Much of our knowledge is transmitted through the schools. Schools can condition children to be whatever it expects; if the school expects nothing, it will get nothing—in most cases. When children receive the right knowledge, the children can carry on and support the tenets of the culture. In this way, we are able to support our own institutions. It should be a two-way process where institutions support individuals and individuals support institutions, thereby

sustaining and maintaining culture and community. Man has many institutions within society. These institutions in society are designed to develop the society to the highest level. Institutions fall into a number of categories: familial, political, economic, social, educational, and religious. Institutions are also designed to promote the development of the individual, the family, the community, and the general society. It is necessary for a family, community, and society to promote the growth and development of its institutions. Usually the community itself, local, county, state, and federal governments are responsible for the development of these institutions. Sometimes such institutions are sponsored by private organizations. Institutions come into being to serve the people. Individuals, the family, the church, organizations in the community and other institutions, should promote and provide for the development of institutions within the community. The individual, the community, the family, and institutions all support and reinforce one another. How can the community grow if there is no institutional support? By the same token, how can institutions grow if the individual, the family, and the community do not support these institutions? Any aware society knows that it takes institutions to provide for the maintenance of the society, and the training of those individuals within the society. Institutions are designed for this purpose. A society will have various institutions set up for this purpose. These institutions are designed to promote the values and culture of the society.

11. **Instill in your children sound values and high moral principles.** Children cannot function without values. Without values and morals, children will not be disciplined. Today the family expects the school, the school expects the church, and the church expects the family to give the children values. Consequently, no one is giving children

a sense of values. At one time, children spent more time around parents, and parents were instrumental in supplying children with values. In these days both parents spend long hours at work, where there are two parents, and don't have time to adequately give them values. We must find a way to instill in our children high morals and sound values.

12. **Give your children a vision for the future and be family oriented.** The family is the most important institution in society. No individual has ever succeeded on a high level without a strong family. Children need to have a decent role model for how one should behave. Without a role model, children have no example of how to grow into mature adulthood. We must also feel positive that we will have the opportunity to grow, live our lives, and be productive citizens. Today some children act as if the world is soon coming to an end, and have no reason to worry about the future. Let me remind you that Plato in 300 B.C. felt the world was coming to an end, because of all the negativity that was prevalent at the time (Plato, 300 B.C., *The Republic*). But it hasn't come to an end yet and likely will not soon come to an end. We must live our lives as if we have a future.

13. **Provide your children with a wholesome education and valuable skills.** Parents should teach children whatever skills the parents possess. At one time parents were more involved in teaching children what skills they had. Lately, we have depended on the schools to provide this training. We need to get back to giving our children whatever advantage we can. At one time parents would provide an apprenticeship for their children, and children would learn the family business within the family. This is not the case in most families today, but we must still find a way to help provide children with an education.

14. **Be more responsible about your relationships.** Because of our conditioning during slavery we are getting away

from the traditional monogamous family model. There are fewer and fewer marriage attachments among Black men and women. Sixty percent of Black families are headed by females. We need to be more careful about how we get in and out of relationships. The monogamous family model has proven effective for nurturing families. We should think about a permanent relationship rather than freely jumping in and out of serial relationships.

15. **Rebuild your communities morally, spiritually, economically, and politically.** What we become is in part because of the community in which we grow and develop. We must all give something back to our communities. If we don't give something back to our communities, we limit their growth and development. No matter how far you venture from home, always support your original community. We all belong to a community of some sort: we should share, help, and reach out to the community; the community of which we are a part, and the larger community. We should give back with our sweat, time, and heart. Take action and make the community a better place. Make time for your community. It'll get you out of yourself, help you and the community to grow, and help you feel connected with others. There are a number of resources any community should have to promote the growth and development of that community. Communities should create living and working environments to enhance the health and living conditions of its members. Such things as recycling, conserving energy or water, landscaping, planting a tree, caring for a garden, getting involved in Little League, Pewee football, or the PTO, the Boy or Girl Scouts, or getting involved in a whole host of community activities are all important. A community should have a variety of community-based organizations, health-care providers, disease-prevention programs, programs for physical activities, nutrition

programs, community centers, parks and recreation, as well as other programs and activities. Communities need such activities for basic growth and development. Treat others in the community as you would like to be treated. Love and compassion should be exhibited toward self and others in the community. Be an agent of good in the community. Think how you can benefit yourself and those in your community (McKay, Forsyth, and Eifert, 2010, *Your Life on Purpose*). *Love thy neighbor as thyself.* Devote yourself to loving those around you. It is necessary for a community to have support from the family, society, and its various institutions in order to function. There are several important aspects of the community: the individual, the family, the school, the church, and the society. The family is most important because it produces the individual; the community is next because the family must function within the context of the community; and the society is last but not least because the family and community must exist within the society. It's important that we develop and maintain a healthy sense of community. Some have gotten away from giving back to the community that basically gave their beginnings. It's good to *move on up,* as was a popular theme with the TV show, "The Jeffersons." But we must give whatever we have to offer to help rebuild, re-establish, and regenerate our communities. We're not all equal in talent, but we all have something we can offer to support and maintain our original communities—even if we move 2,000 miles away. We must share whatever unique talent or ability we have. We shouldn't go through life buying trinkets, stereos, big-screen TV's, clothes, and cars, etc. These things have a place, but we must have a higher calling for our finances. All of us can see the daily destruction in our communities: dilapidated buildings, drugs, school dropouts, suicides and homicides, drive-bys, murders, rapes, robberies, teenage pregnancies, AIDS, single-parent families, and many other problems. It doesn't have to be monumental; it can be something simple that you give. We must elevate the status of the community (since many institutions should exist within any community) to that of an institution and take care of one of the fundamental reasons for being; to build that institution that figuratively gave birth to us—the community. A healthy sense of community is the cornerstone of a modern democracy. We can't maintain a healthy sense of community if we fail to give back and continue to allow our communities to deteriorate. We can't grow any bigger than our communities, and our communities determine the limits of our creativity. The truth is our lives aren't really about us. Our lives are bout everyone our lives touch. Every life is connected to every other life. We must be sure that we promote the development of our communities. Ask yourself how can I better the lives of those in my community?

16. **We must change our language structure**. African Americans will have difficulty in changing the language structure of this country. However, it will be necessary for us to be careful about the way we use words from the English language. Other groups, at times, use words to have different meanings than what African Americans understand them to mean. Other groups are good at the semantics of the language, since it is their language, and they have spent years studying it. Often, words and their meaning determine how we structure and view things. Podiar (1967, p. 39) in *How Bigotry Builds through Language*, felt that "Language as a potent force of our society goes beyond being merely a communication device. Language not only expresses ideas and concepts but may actually shape them. Often the process is completely unconscious with the individual concerned unaware of the influence of the spoken or written expression upon his thought process."

We must be deliberate about not allowing negativity in the structure of the language to influence the way we see and view our situation. Since other groups are primarily responsible for the structure of the English language, it is axiomatic that there are certainly some built-in prejudices in the language. Frantz Fanon (1967, pp. 17-18) in *Black Skin, White Mask* stated, "To speak means to be in a position to use a certain syntax, to grasp the morphology of this or that language, but it means above all to assume a culture, to support the weight of civilization. A man who has a language consequently possesses the world expressed by that language." For example, usage of the word non-white is meant mainly to exclude Blacks from the mainstream. It is a way of differentiating between those of other groups' origin and Blacks. However, it has a built-in prejudice and contradiction. If white is the absence of color, how can black be considered non-white. It would be more logical to say white is non-black, since white is the absence of color. Also, the word white is structured in the English language so that the word automatically means something positive, whereas black usually means something negative. For example, blackmail, black sheep, blackball, and blacklist all connote something negative.

17. **Develop strong leadership**. We need strong leadership in our families and otherwise. We are getting to the point where young men are afraid of taking leadership roles. They are afraid the same thing will happen to them that happened to Martin Luther King, Jr. and Malcolm X. We must have leaders who are not afraid. These leaders must be instilled with the appropriate leadership values that will sustain us. We must produce many leaders, so that if one is destroyed, another will come to the fore. There is also a need for leadership with strong character.

18. **Tell our story**. We must continue to tell our story, and not let the history of our people die. It is necessary to keep the history of our culture live among the people. Each family must also keep its own history alive. This allows people to know who we are, and where we came from. This gives us a sense of continuity.

19. **Become more spiritual than religious**. Many people believe in a blonde haired, blue-eyed Jesus. It is necessary to see our God in an image like ourselves. We must believe in living a righteous, balanced, just, and reciprocal life; rather than living according to principals based on allegories, fables, myth, and folktales.

20. **Modeling**. We must learn to model our lives for our families. We must live as an example for the way we want our children to live. We must live a life that our children can exemplify. We must live in such a way as to have our children to do as we do and not as we say. Doing one thing and teaching children to do another is not a feasible way to live.

21. **Racial education**. We must teach our children about racism and its effects on us as a people. Such education gives children a strong base for surviving in this society. To live in such a racist society without such information is cultural suicide.

22. **Take control of self**. Learn to control your anger. You can't make sound decisions while angry. You also can't think rationally while angry. Choose your battles: you can't afford to expend a tremendous amount of wasted energy. Always consider your options, you always have positive options.

23. **Build our self-esteem**. Work daily at building your self-esteem. Focus on the positive, and don't worry about the negative. Create value in yourself on a daily basis: do something worthwhile for yourself and others. Get rid of

false notions about yourself: try to feel good about yourself. Focus on your strengths rather than your weaknesses.

24. **We need to understand the differences between people, celebrate them, learn to integrate these differences, and become a true world community.**

These are only a few of the things one can do to rid the family of the Post-Traumatic Slave Syndrome. If you accomplish these things, you will have made significant strides.

Epilogue

As a result of my family dysfunction, the only boys in the family who graduated from high school were Jack and I: the others didn't have much choice, my mother and father not caring much about promoting or providing for their children's education. Three of the girls graduated high school: Sarah, Debra, and Betty. Sam my oldest brother, turned out to be a truck driver; Lucille my oldest sister, never worked to my knowledge; I'm not sure what Martha did as a vocation; Betty never held down a job; Lewis never held a worthwhile job; John was a construction worker for most of his life; Sarah worked for a while at some menial tasks; Jack went from one menial job to another; and Debra did menial jobs for a short part of her life. I got a Bachelor's degree in sociology, a Master's degree in counseling, a Master's degree in social work, and worked on a Ph.D. at two different Midwestern universities. Even with my degrees, my background made it difficult to hold on to a job. I worked for a number of years but ended up going on disability.

Again, because of our dysfunction most of my family members weren't very close. I was closest to my sister Debra and my brother John. Most of them had left home by the time I developed my conscious level. Sam, Jack, Lewis, Betty, John, and Lucille are deceased. Sam died of cranial cancer; it was reported that Jack committed suicide; Lewis was run over by a car; John died of natural causes; Betty also died of natural causes, and my oldest sister Lucille died of lung cancer. Of course, my mother and father are deceased.

My family members who are still living all live in Texas. I live in a Chicago suburb. I rarely see family members because I don't like to fly, and I am not in good enough physical condition to drive. I have severe pain in my back and legs. I hadn't seen any of my sisters and brothers since my mother's funeral in 1988. Family members were slow to even speak to me. I have since the funeral talked to several of my sisters by phone.

None of my family members lacked intelligence. Had it not been for their history, I believe all could have made a meaningful contribution to society. It must be said though that most of my nieces and nephews, and great nieces and nephews were able to make significant intergenerational progress. I drive a decent car and live in a decent house. I have a wife and two sons. My oldest son graduated college and found a home in California. The youngest is still trying to find his way. My wife and I are both retired.

Both my father and mother died broken in mind, body, and spirit. My parents never accomplished any meaningful objectives, except to bring a partially dysfunctional family into the world. This was in part due to the Post-Traumatic Slave Syndrome. My sisters and brothers had similar results. Only in the last generation have we begun to see some positive results in our family's social, economic, psychological, and educational attitude and behavior.

We have objectively examined some aspects of the Post-Traumatic Slave Syndrome and presented some specific solutions. It should not be difficult to grasp the intensity of this programming process, and how it has promoted this syndrome in the African American family. Each day the news is permeated with information about the deterioration of our families. The African American family is in a state of war, and it won't get better simply by doing nothing. The time for action is now! Each family member must be responsible for deprogramming him/herself. Contrary to popular opinion, things have not improved for the masses of people. African American families should not delude themselves into thinking that things are going well. A large percentage of our families are presently experiencing serious difficulties, very similar to those experienced during earlier invasions of Africa. Things have improved for a few individuals, but the system is designed that way. We must ensure that the overwhelming majority of our families are strong for the twenty-first century. Without a strong and viable family, we cannot expect to have well-functioning individuals. Without well-functioning individuals, we cannot expect to have strong and viable families.

When Black folks get tired of other groups, and other groups get tired of Black folks, the moral ark of the universe will fall across the sky, and we all will have no choice but to change our behavior. At this point, we continue to blame one another for the problems of society.

About the Author

JAY THOMAS WILLIS is a graduate of the University of Houston, Houston, Texas, where he earned a Masters' degree in social work; he is also a graduate of the Masters' degree counselling program at Texas Southern University, Houston, Texas. He attended undergraduate school at Stephen F. Austin State University, Nacogdoches, Texas, where he earned a B.S. degree in sociology and social and rehabilitative services.

He worked as a Clinical Social Worker for seventeen years, providing direct clinical services as well as supervision. He has been a consultant to a nursing home and a boys' group home; taught college courses in sociology, family, and social work in community college and university settings; and has worked as a family therapist for several agencies in the Chicago area. In addition, he was a consultant to a number of home-health care agencies in the south suburbs and Chicago. Mr. Willis is a past CHAMPUS peer reviewer for the American Psychological Association and the American Psychiatric Association. He also spent a number of years in private practice as a Licensed Clinical Social Worker in the State of Illinois.

Mr. Willis has traveled and lectured extensively on the condition of the African American community. He has written twenty-six books, and written many journal articles on the subject of the African American community. He has written several magazine articles. He has also written Op-Ed Commentaries for the *Chicago Defender, Final Call, East Side Daily News* of Cleveland, and *Dallas Examiner.* He currently lives in Richton Park, Illinois with his wife and son.

Printed in the United States
By Bookmasters